0072276

Pilot's Avionics Survival Guide

TAB
PRACTICAL
FLYING SERIES

Other books in the TAB Practical Flying Series

Pilot's Avionics Survival Guide

Edward R. Maher

Edited by Matt Thurber

TAB Books
Division of McGraw-Hill, Inc.
Blue Ridge Summit, PA 17294-0850

FIRST EDITION
FIRST PRINTING

Library of Congress Cataloging-in-Publication Data

Maher, Ed.
   Pilot's avionics survival guide : / by Ed Maher.
      p.   cm.
   Includes index.
   ISBN 0-8306-4205-6   ISBN 0-8306-4204-8 (pbk.)
   1. Avionics—Maintenance and repair. 2. Aeronautics—Safety measures. I. Title.
   TL695.M34 1993
   629.135'028'8—dc20   93-8051
                                                            CIP

Acquisitions Editor: Jeff Worsinger
Editorial Team: Lisa A. Doyle, Editor
               Joanne Slike, Executive Editor
Production team: Katherine G. Brown, Director
               Brenda S. Wilhide, Layout
               Rhonda E. Baker, Coding
               Jana L. Fisher, Coding
               Ollie Harmon, Coding
               Lisa M. Mellott, Coding
               Brenda M. Plasterer, Coding
               Tina M. Sourbier, Coding
               Joann Woy, Indexer
Design team: Jaclyn J. Boone, Designer
               Brian Allison, Associate Designer
Cover design by Paul Saberin, Farm Out Graphics, Chambersburg, Pa.   PFS
Cover photograph courtesy of Rockwell.   4264

This book is dedicated to the memory of my son, Steven E. H. Maher and to his son, David S. Maher, without whose support, this book would not have been written.

Contents

Introduction

I FLY A LOT ON BUSINESS, AND I'VE ALSO BEEN ON A LOT OF TEST FLIGHTS with my customers and technicians. Every time I go up, I'm putting my life on the line, trusting that the airplane I'm flying is in excellent condition. That means all Airworthiness Directives are complied with, inspections are done regularly, repairs have been made properly, and of increasing importance these days, the avionics are in tip-top shape.

The air traffic control system is becoming increasingly complex, and users of the system depend more and more on reliable avionics to maintain a proper level of safety. While you can still fly from the east to the west coast VFR and without talking to anyone on the radio in an airplane without an electrical system, most pilots find that a modest amount of reliable avionics is necessary for their flying needs. The number of instrument-rated pilots is growing, and TCAs in major metropolitan areas are surrounded by airspace requiring transponders with mode C altitude reporting capability.

To fly an airplane in these busy areas, reliable avionics is a must. A flight school with unreliable radios will soon lose all of its customers. After a few attempted flights where tower controllers tell you that your communications radio is weak and unreadable, I guarantee you'll wish you'd spent the extra money on that good radio when you had the chance.

But there's more to it than simple communications. The entire ATC system is dependent on reliable avionics. Imagine the confusion if transponders on all the IFR traffic flowing into the San Francisco Bay area suddenly became intermittent. Or what if one airline neglected to ensure the accuracy of its mode C systems for, say, a year? The results would be massive confusion with a much greater potential for near-midair or midair collisions.

Every pilot and aircraft owner participating in the modern ATC system has a responsibility to ensure that the avionics they use are working properly. The best way to do this is to learn the language of avionics, what makes them work, how to communicate with technicians, how to write up a discrepancy, how to perform initial troubleshooting, and the regulations that apply to avionics.

Learning about avionics will not only help you fly safer, but it will enhance your status in the field of aviation by showing the professionals—technicians, controllers, other pilots—that you take the responsibility of safe flying very seriously. Another important benefit is that you will save money, lots of it. With avionics shop rates ranging well over $50 per hour, performing some initial troubleshooting yourself can save you hundreds of dollars. You'll also save by being more well informed when it comes time to upgrade your instrument panel. And when you are getting quotes for the upgrade, you'll know which questions to ask to find out why one shop wants an extra $500 for that navcom installation compared to another low-budget shop down the road.

You don't have to own an aircraft to benefit from reading this book. Many pilots rely on rental fleets, and it's not uncommon to find avionics in rental airplanes lacking. By reading this book, you'll learn to recognize reliable equipment and learn more about how to operate it. You'll also learn simple ways to deal with inflight problems and how to help your flying club maintain its planes' radios by writing clear squawk descriptions. There is nothing more disappointing than scheduling an airplane for a flight, then getting the engine started and finding out that the only com radio is inoperative. Think how much happier you'll be if you can troubleshoot the problem, replace the defective microphone with the spare you always carry, and enjoy that sunny Sunday flight.

This book is also intended to help those of you who are building that dream airplane in your garage. You no doubt have a bunch of questions about what avionics to buy, how to install them, and how to maintain them after you finish your airplane. This book will give you a head start and help you make all those decisions. After you get your bird flying, keep this book as a handy reference for dealing with any avionics problems that crop up.

Remember to have fun while reading this book. After all, isn't that why most of us are in this business? I've been involved with airplanes for over 30 years. I started in the Air Force and then spent 23 years with Beech Aircraft in a variety of avionics-related positions including avionics testing on Beech's revolutionary all-composite Starship twin turboprop. I've been writing about avionics since 1984 and have been featured in a number of magazines including *Avionics News*, where I'm a contributing editor, *Kitplanes*, *Aviation Equipment Maintenance*, *Avionics*, and *Rotor & Wing*. My first two books are entitled *A Pilot's Checklist* and *Best Shop Practices* (for avionics technicians). After leaving Beech Aircraft, I worked as Avionics Manager for Crownair, an FBO based at Montgomery Field in San Diego, California. During that job, I was faced with the problems and solutions outlined in this book every day, and it always amazed me how much aircraft owners could save if they just knew a little bit about avionics. I wrote this book to help you learn how to deal with these problems, save money, and keep on flying.

This book isn't intended to teach you how to solder a new resistor onto the circuit board of your expensive King navcom, nor is it an in-depth course in avionics fundamentals. You bought this book to help eliminate the uncertainties and mystique behind avionics repairs. The more you know about what's going on under your instrument panel, the better and safer your flying will be. The more you know about what needs to be done when there is a problem, the more time and money you'll save.

There is one important thing you must do to help make this book truly useful when you have a problem. Not all repairs are simple, but being familiar with how the radio works and recognizing when and how it failed will greatly aid the technician. Learn as much as you can from the user's manual for your equipment, and keep a squawk diary of all problems you encounter with your avionics, especially intermittent problems. This information could prove to be very valuable when the technician is trying to track down an elusive problem.

Each chapter in this book covers one avionics system. After a brief description of the system, I list installation tips for that particular system. These are considerations you should discuss with your avionics installer to make sure the job is done to the highest standards and to your satisfaction. This is followed by a section on basic troubleshooting, which details problems you're likely to encounter.

If you're in the middle of a problem right now, jump to that chapter and you'll learn how to identify the problem and do some basic troubleshooting. Keep careful notes in your squawk diary and set aside some time to discuss the problem with your technician. If the problem is intermittent, you may have to try and duplicate the conditions under which the failure occurred. If you aren't faced with a problem yet, just sit down and enjoy this book and learn as much as you can.

1
Rules to fly by

GREG WAS PROUD OF HIS NEW AIRPLANE. WELL, IT WASN'T REALLY NEW, but it was a well-preserved 1978 Beech Debonair with a low-time engine and a full suite of modern King avionics including an intercom and a Northstar loran. It was the perfect cross-country, IFR machine . . . not that he had his IFR rating yet, but at least he now had a great airplane for learning, and he wouldn't have to spend any more money on avionics.

The previous owner gave Greg a quick checkout after they signed all the papers. The prepurchase inspection had taken a little longer than expected and the owner had insisted on taking Greg to his favorite local restaurant, so it wasn't until late afternoon that Greg was able to take off for home. The owner had assured him that all necessary maintenance had been taken care of. The airplane did fly well and the engine sounded sweet, so Greg trusted him and planned his flight back to his home base. He figured he'd arrive just shortly before dark, plenty of time to avoid the mountains surrounding the open valley where the airport was situated.

As he neared home, Greg contacted ATC for flight following. He listened to the ATIS for his home base and set his altimeter. Funny, the new altimeter setting changed his altitude by 300 feet. Greg pondered that for a few seconds, then shrugged and descended to get back to 3000 feet, which is the altitude he reported when he first called.

Greg was following the familiar route, the highway, which had enough traffic to see its outline in the dark fields that surrounded it. He was busy looking down at the highway when suddenly all the lights on the cars disappeared. Looking up, Greg saw nothing, just a blank gray wall where the windshield met the outside air. After a quick scan of the panel, Greg's eyes latched onto the attitude indicator. He immediately began thinking of what to do. Turn around? Keep going and hope that he'd bust out of the cloud on the other side? He tried to look at his chart, but the combination of dim red cockpit light and the need to keep his eyes on the attitude indicator to stay right side up made consulting the chart too difficult.

Where exactly am I? Greg wondered. He knew the area pretty well, but he also knew there were mountain peaks over 2500 feet in the area. He started a shallow turn to the left but then realized that most of the mountains were in that direction. He didn't think there were any obstacles to the right, so he reversed direction and began a 180-degree turn to the right. He didn't dare lose any altitude, not being 100-percent sure about where he was in relation to the mountains. Nervously, he continued the turn, also aware that the higher speed of the Debonair was something he wasn't used to. The thought that the larger the radius of a turn, the faster you fly briefly occurred to Greg, but he banished those thoughts and concentrated on keeping the airplane in the turn.

Shortly after leveling off, a call came in from ATC: "Three-four bravo, do you need vectors to your destination?"

Greg didn't reply; he was too busy flying.

The controller called again. Greg was just about to transmit a quick "standby" when he broke out of the clouds and saw the freeway below him. "Whew," he sighed, and called the controller and said he was turning to avoid some clouds and would be descending to 2000 feet.

"Three four bravo, let me know if you need vectors, and be aware, there is high terrain to the west of your position," the controller said.

Greg descended to 2000 feet above the freeway and turned back towards home. When he arrived, he contacted the tower and set himself up for a slightly larger than normal pattern so he could adjust to the faster speed of the Debonair. *Strange,* Greg thought while on downwind, *it sure seems lower when you're this far out.* He continued to fly the familiar pattern, and once on final, double-checked that the gear was down and locked and added full flaps. It was dark now, but Greg felt confident because he'd flown at night many times at this airport and had made sure he was night current. He was used to flying by the seat of his pants during this phase, so he only glanced occasionally at the airspeed indicator during the landing but otherwise kept his eyes scanning outside the cockpit.

On the ground, Greg turned off at the end of the runway to keep from having to use brakes too much, then stopped and retracted the flaps and asked ground control for permission to taxi to his new tiedown.

It wasn't until he had the airplane shutdown and was logging the Hobbs time that Greg noticed the altimeter. His homebase airport's elevation was 350 feet AGL. The altimeter read 600 feet. Greg's heart started hammering as he realized that not only was that the reason why he'd appeared to be so low on downwind, but that he was a lot lower than he thought he was when he entered that cloud and did the 180-degree turn.

Thinking it through, Greg figured that the altimeter was way out of calibration, and he hadn't detected it because he took off from an uncontrolled field and never got a local altimeter setting. When he reset the altimeter on the way home, he should have paid attention when he had to adjust it so much.

Later at home, Greg took a closer look at the logbooks for his new airplane. He tried to remember if the mechanic who did the prepurchase inspection said anything about the static system. Wasn't it supposed to get checked every two years? There it was: last year it had the inspection done per FAR 91.413.

Altimeter system, encoding altimeter, and transponder certification being done on a Swearingen Merlin per FAR 91.411 and 91.413.

Greg pulled out his FAR book and looked it up. *Wait a minute. That's for transponders and encoders. Static systems is FAR 91.411.* He looked and looked, but the last entry he could find for a static system check was 10 years ago. After thinking about that for a moment, Greg remembered the guy who sold him the Debonair had said he flew only VFR and hardly ever took it on trips. *Maybe he didn't think static system checks are required for VFR*, Greg thought.

Thinking through the whole episode again, Greg realized that he made a few basic mistakes that, added together, could have cost him his life. First, he should have looked at the logbooks more closely. Second, he needed to learn more about the regulations now that he was an airplane owner; things were getting more complicated. Third, he should have stayed overnight, gotten a fresh start the next morning, and not been in such a hurry. That way he might not have forgotten to check his altimeter against the local setting and would have seen the 300-foot error before he took off. He also would have had more time to read the POH and logbooks to get to know his new airplane better. Greg kept his Debonair parked until he could get the static check done and take care of the rest of the squawks from the prepurchase inspection.

THE RULES

If Greg had simply called Flight Service and set his altimeter to the local setting, he would have noticed that his altimeter exceeded the FAA limits of 75-foot accuracy. With the altimeter set to the local altimeter setting, your altimeter should not read more than 75 feet high or low compared to field elevation.

Although it might not seem like it, FARs do require accurate altimeters at all times, whether you are flying VFR or IFR. The FAR that specifies the static system test, 91.411, requires the test be done every two years in order to operate an airplane in controlled airspace under IFR. But what if you fly only VFR like Greg? Would you feel safe with an altimeter reading 300 off? How about if it reads 300 feet high, so you always think you are flying 300 feet higher than you actually are? Such inaccuracy tends to chip away at your safety margins.

When your airplane was built, it had to meet certain requirements to be certified. To remain airworthy, it must meet additional requirements, one of which is that all equipment installed in the airplane must work properly at all times. While there are exceptions to this rule, detailed in FAR 91.213, certain essential items like altimeters are not included. FAR 91.405 states that among the required inspections, all discrepancies must be repaired. Therefore, in the absence of an official rule stating that the altimeter must be accurate, you can infer from FAR 91.405 that all installed equipment must work properly, and an airplane with an inaccurate altimeter is unairworthy.

Let's go over that again. FAR 91.405 states that between all required inspections like the annual inspection, all inoperative items must be repaired. Before the FAA enacted a rule change a few years ago, that regulation essentially meant that no one was allowed to fly with inoperative equipment. Every single item in the airplane had to be working, from the landing light to the transponder, whether or not you needed that item for the flight you were planning. Most people didn't pay too much attention to that rule until the FAA tightened up its enforcement procedures and started going after operators, mostly charter companies, for discrepancies like broken clocks or inoperative landing lights. When word spread that the FAA was taking a hard line on interpretation of FAR 91.405, people in the aviation industry and industry trade groups asked the FAA if the rules could be altered slightly. It seemed ridiculous to have to cancel a day flight for a blown landing light if a new bulb wasn't available immediately.

The FAA responded with subparagraph (d)(2) of FAR 91.213, which allows pilots to fly an airplane with inoperative equipment, as long as certain conditions are met. These include "that the inoperative instruments and equipment are not:

(i) Part of the VFR-day type certification instruments and equipment prescribed in the applicable airworthiness regulations under which the aircraft was type certificated;

(ii) Indicated as required on the aircraft's equipment list, or on the Kinds of Operations Equipment List for the kind of flight operations being conducted;

(iii) Required by [FAR] 91.205 or any other rule of this part for the specific kind of flight operation being conducted; or

(iv) Required to be operational by an airworthiness directive."

The regulation goes on to discuss that if one of the specified unnecessary pieces of equipment is inoperative and is not required for the flight, you must placard the item as inoperative. In some cases, you might be required to disable the equipment, in which case the action that was taken to disable the equipment must be logged in the maintenance records. Sometimes, the work to disable equipment can be done only by a licensed technician. What you can and can't do mechanically is discussed later in this chapter.

The new rule makes it easier to determine what broken equipment you can fly with. Basically, all you have to do is refer to FAR 91.205. As long as the broken equipment isn't on that list, you can fly. Of course you still have to placard and/or disable to broken equipment.

During day VFR flight, for example, you must have the following working items:

- airspeed indicator
- altimeter
- magnetic-direction indicator
- tachometer
- oil pressure gauge
- oil temperature gauge
- fuel quantity gauge, etc.

Even though it isn't avionics, if your airplane was certified with an electric fuel pump (like a Piper Seminole) then part of the required equipment is the fuel pressure gauge. Even though the fuel pressure gauge isn't listed on the 91.205 list for minimum equipment required for VFR flight, you still can't fly without a working fuel pressure gauge for each engine since the fuel pressure gauge was required as a condition of original certification. In other words, merely referring to FAR 91.205 can get you into trouble if you use it as a quasi-minimum equipment list.

You also might have heard about minimum equipment lists (MELs) used by some charter and corporate operators. Forget it. You don't want to get involved in this hassle. FAA does permit operations of certain aircraft for which a master MEL has been prepared with certain inoperative equipment. But you don't need to get involved in that, as a closer reading of FAR 91.213 will show. Larger aircraft have different rules, mainly because they have so much more equipment to deal with. So FAA publishes master MELs for airplanes like corporate jets, large twins, and turboprops. The operators of these aircraft take the master MEL and come up with a customized MEL that applies specifically to their aircraft. After getting this approved by the local FSDO— not a quick process—the operators are then permitted to fly with equipment items that are listed on their approved MEL being inoperative. It's basically a more complex form of what we're allowed to do on a simple airplane, a more formal method of placarding inoperative equipment.

This whole discussion started over an inaccurate altimeter. Because we've established that a working, accurate altimeter is essential and required, even for VFR flight, you have no choice if your altimeter becomes inaccurate. You must have it fixed and cannot fly until it reads accurately.

RECURRING EVENTS

Let's go over the avionics items you need to worry about on a regular basis:

- Your airplane should have an altimeter/static system test, even if you don't fly IFR. This is the simplest way to keep your static system and altimeter accurate, and it only costs about $50 every two years. Reference FAR 91.411.

Warning! Don't forget to remove tape from static ports after altimeter system testing. The tape is required for the test.

- The transponder and encoder must be tested every two years per FAR 91.413. This test checks the transponder output and the accuracy of the encoding altimeter. Cost: about $100 every two years.

- ELT battery must be replaced at intervals marked on the battery. Usually you can buy a two- or three-year battery. I recommend the two-year battery because that way someone will be looking at your ELT more frequently, and if the old battery leaks, you'll find out sooner. Later, this book discusses how to test ELTs so you don't get caught with a dead one when you need it most.

- VOR check is due every 30 days. The easiest way to do this is to find a check point over which you fly near your home base. Then simply perform the test at least once a month or more frequently, just to be sure you're always legal. You may want to log this in a separate avionics log where you keep track of all avionics work done on your airplane.

- Aircraft radio station license is due each five years. This is an easy one to forget, but you must keep track of it and renew this license every five years.

- Vacuum filters. See chapter 20 for a more detailed discussion of vacuum filters. There are usually two filters in most light aircraft: a central vacuum filter that needs to be changed every 500 hours, and a vacuum regulator filter that gets changed every 100 hours.

How do you keep track of all these events? There is the annual inspection every year, the static/transponder test, the ELT battery, VOR check, perhaps some recurring airworthiness directives and service bulletins, radio station license, vacuum filters, your medical certificate, biennial flight review, and your IFR currency.

The simplest way to keep track is use a day planner. If you're not already in that habit, you can pick up a simple calendar/planner at an office supply store and use it exclusively for your aviation tracking. Whenever you complete an event, make a note of when the next one is due. It's that simple. For instance, when Greg has his static/transponder check done on his new Debonair, say, in August 1993, all he has to do is make a note in the long-term planning section of the planner for August 1995 that the Debonair's static/transponder check is due. The same would go with the ELT battery. When you install a new one, note the date when it must be replaced in your planner and you'll never forget it. Another useful idea is to note when all these items are due next to the signoff for the annual inspection. That way you'll be forced to make sure you don't miss any items that are coming up soon.

Don't try to rely on memory for these important events. It's too easy to forget to write it down: then one day—surprise—it's been a year since your biennial flight review was due. If you're using a computer to keep track of your flight hours, you can probably plug in the due dates for the static/transponder test, ELT battery, VOR check, and other recurring maintenance events.

Don't forget FAR 91.403 (a): "The owner or operator of an aircraft is primarily responsible for maintaining that aircraft in an airworthy condition . . .."

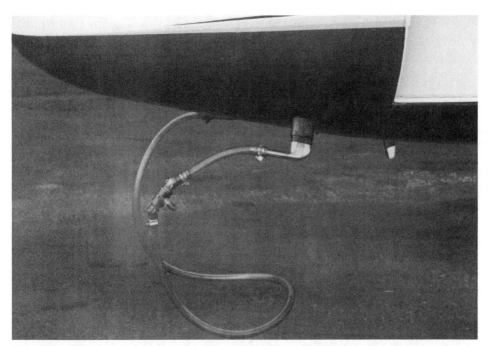

Pitot tube hose connections, part of altimeter system certification per FAR 91.411.

During annual inspection, the inspector found the static system violated. The line was left disconnected and became kinked. The line not only must be replaced, but the static system will have to be tested to verify integrity.

The owner who sold Greg the Debonair sold an unairworthy airplane because the altimeter was inaccurate. Was it the responsibility of that owner's mechanic to make sure the airplane was airworthy? Was it the mechanic who did the prepurchase inspection? No, it was the owner's responsibility, and his noncompliance with the regulations nearly cost Greg his life.

HOW TO SQUAWK A PROBLEM

Remember science and math classes in high school? The teachers drummed into your brain that more than half the solution to a problem lay in defining the problem first. This is also necessary when troubleshooting avionics.

Your goal in squawking a problem is to give the avionics technician enough information so that the tech can zero in on the problem and get right to work fixing it and not spend a bunch of your money doing what you could have done. Keep a notebook handy whenever flying so you can make notes that will speed along the troubleshooting process.

Step one is to isolate the problem. Is it intermittent or does it happen all the time? Are the circumstances the same each time it happens? If there are two of the malfunctioning item, is the other one working normally? Are you sure you are using the equipment properly? Note the conditions of flight during which the problem appeared, including altitude, position, attitude, atmospheric conditions, other avionics status (on or off), other electrical equipment status, or whether engine speed or retractable landing gear operation affects the problem.

Second, spend some of your own time checking for obvious defects such as broken wires, loose connectors, poor bonding (especially at antennas), excess harness stress on connectors at the back of the radio stack, or moisture leaking onto radios. If it's a com problem have you tried the spare microphone?

Your input is valuable and will go a long way towards solving problems. If the technicians insist they can't duplicate the problem you discovered, consider taking one of them for a test flight so you can show them the problem. Obviously you'll want to make sure you can duplicate the problem for their benefit.

KEEPING UP WITH MODS, BULLETINS, AND AIRWORTHINESS DIRECTIVES

Like any part of your airplane, your avionics are potential sources of airworthiness directives (ADs) and manufacturers' service information like service bulletins and letters.

An AD will reference serial numbers of the equipment to which it applies. If you get an AD in the mail, check the serial number applicability, and if it doesn't apply, make a note on the AD and put it in your aircraft records.

You probably won't hear too much about manufacturers' service information unless you contact the manufacturer and ask to be put on the mailing list for new bulletins. In some cases, this could cost money for an annual subscription fee. But your avionics shop, if a dealer for your brand of avionics, will receive bulletins and letters from the manufacturer. It is up to the shop manager to notify you if a particular bulletin might apply to one of your radios.

In some cases, the suggested modifications are not important, but in other cases, a bulletin could be directly applicable to a problem you are having. When you bring your airplane in for service, you might ask the shop manager to let you know if there are any service bulletins or letters applying to your equipment that should be taken care of or that cover the problem you are having. Keeping your avionics up to date with the latest mods and upgrades will make them last longer and increase their long-term value. Don't ignore manufacturers' service information.

Keep in mind that ADs are mandatory and must be complied with. Manufacturers' service information is always optional, no matter what the manufacturer tells you, unless specified as being required for compliance with an AD.

2
Technicians and certification

I T IS NOT THE INTENT OF THIS BOOK TO TEACH YOU HOW TO DELVE INTO the innards of your airplane's black boxes and solder a new transistor on a deeply buried circuit board. You'll get the most from this book if you use the knowledge to help you isolate and troubleshoot problems to get them fixed quicker and cheaper. The bottom line is that you'll need to establish a good working relationship with avionics technicians. Who are these mysterious people?

Most technicians have spent years and years training and retraining, just for the privilege of getting their hands on those expensive black boxes. First, to work on any kind of transmitter, a technician must be licensed by the Federal Communications Commission (FCC). While it is possible to simply learn what is necessary to take and pass the test, most technicians have a degree in electronics or a lot of training in electronic repair and maintenance. One good way of getting this experience, for instance, is in the military.

You'll frequently find technicians at avionics shops split into a few specialty areas. Bench techs are the people who dig into the black boxes after they've been removed from the aircraft. Bench technicians also specialize. One will work mostly on pulse-type equipment (DME or transponders), while another will be the shop's autopilot guru. Other technicians might specialize in areas like installation, troubleshooting, and customer service. Some large shops, for example, have a person assigned to work with customers on troubleshooting avionics, sometimes flying with the customer to isolate problems before radios are removed for repair. It's a lot more efficient to troubleshoot first than to waste a $70-per-hour technician's time opening up a black box that isn't broken. Also, as you'll learn, there are many problems that are due to installation factors and that must be examined with the radio installed, looking at the system as a whole.

Bench techs must have the FCC certification to work on transmitters like com radios. For all other radios, a tech must be a licensed FAA airframe mechanic, hold an FAA Repairman's Certificate covering the specific type of work, or work for an FAA-approved repair station. To install avionics, a technician must be either a licensed Airframe Mechanic, hold an FAA Repairman's Certificate for installation work, or simply work for an FAA-approved repair station. There is as yet no formal FAA certification for avionics technicians, although many airframe and powerplant (A&P) schools do offer separate avionics courses leading to FCC certification and usually including FAA Airframe Mechanic certification.

AVIONICS SHOP CERTIFICATION

Most avionics shops are FAA-approved repair stations. An owner of a shop has two choices when it comes to legal status: The owner can either elect to go the non-FAA-approved route, or seek approval.

Lack of FAA approval simply means the shop isn't an official repair station. To operate with repair station status, the shop must apply for and be approved as a repair station by the local FAA Flight Standards District Office (FSDO). This involves showing proof of meeting certain requirements such as experience of management, ability to install and repair various types of avionics, commitment to stocking spare parts and necessary test and repair equipment (including calibrated tools). Other requirements might include providing a clean room for instrument repairs or recurrent training for technicians.

Many avionics shops seek official repair station status because not only does it ensure customers that the shop meets a minimum, verifiable set of FAA standards, but it also allows the shop to hire nonlicensed individuals to do the actual work. There is no exception to the requirement for an FCC-licensed tech to work on transmitters, but a repair station can technically hire anyone off the street and put them to work doing whatever work the repair station is authorized for. This does not mean that a non-licensed installer working for a repair station is less qualified than an FAA-licensed airframe mechanic working for a nonapproved avionics shop. In fact, because of the stringent requirements attached to repair stations, the people who work there receive lots of training and are very well qualified for the work they do.

Many repair stations like to hire FAA airframe and powerplant mechanics anyway because of the excellent training they receive, and most shops employ FCC-licensed individuals for bench work.

Technically, a licensed airframe mechanic is the only person allowed to remove and install a radio unless the shop is a repair station. Yes, this means simply removing a radio from an instrument panel, which usually requires a twist of a screw. The aircraft owner is not allowed to remove the radio, nor can a bench tech who is not an airframe mechanic.

For a non-FAA-approved shop, then, each person who works there must be appropriately licensed. The airframe mechanic removes and install avionics for the bench techs to repair; the bench tech who is not an airframe mechanic must perform repairs under the supervision of one who is. The bench tech gives the repaired radio back to the airframe mechanic for reinstallation. The airframe mechanic would have to perform all the harness building, wiring, and physical installation work for a new installation. A licensed airframe and powerplant mechanic holding FAA Inspection Authorization (IA) would have to sign off the FAA form 337 to make the installation legal.

This would obviously be an inefficient way to run an avionics shop. You'll find shops that do operate like this, where the bench tech removes and installs the radios being worked on, and nonlicensed personnel assist on installations. Technically this is illegal, but it does happen. I mention this not to sic the FAA on a bunch of rule-breakers, but to let you know that some shops might not be complying with the greater percentage of the rules. Typically, the more a shop complies with the rules and shows a willingness to work with the FAA, the better the quality of their work.

Repair station status confers certain benefits on avionics shops. While it does involve more surveillance by FAA inspectors and more stringent recordkeeping, earning a repair station certificate more than makes up for the increased paperwork by allowing improved efficiency. To obtain a repair station certificate, the owner of an avionics shop must meet certain minimum requirements. These include:

- hiring personnel with a minimum specified amount of experience
- setting up procedures for handling repairs, processing parts, maintaining test equipment
- recurrent employee training

When a company has a repair station certificate, it need not hire licensed personnel to perform the work. Standards are set by the FAA, and the heads of the various departments in the shop are responsible for enforcing those standards. A repair station, for instance, can hire an unlicensed avionics installer. Just because this person does not have an airframe mechanic license does not mean he or she is not qualified to do the work. There are many installers, for instance, who formerly worked for airframe manufacturers and never obtained their airframe license; they would be ideal candidates for installation work at avionics shops.

The head of the installation department oversees all the work done in that department and ensures that it meets company and FAA quality standards. The FAA requires that each repair station employ an experienced inspector to maintain quality levels. Essentially, the unlicensed personnel are being guided by the experienced inspector and department heads.

Another benefit is that the repair station transfers the burden of paperwork from the person who did the job to the managers. At a nonapproved shop, each licensed person who did the work would be required to fill out logbooks, Form 337s, and weight-and-balance updates. At a repair station, management is responsible for all the paperwork, leaving the technical personnel free to install and fix radios and keep the revenue stream flowing in the right direction. This points out another drawback to the nonapproved shop. In reality, most mechanics hate paperwork and gladly leave it for managers to fill out. Technically, this is not legal. The person who does the work must fill out and sign the logbooks, but you'll rarely find this in the field.

This long explanation has been to simply introduce you to the types of shops you're likely to run into. Chapter 3 includes tips on how to deal effectively with your avionics shop and what to look for when you're evaluating a new one. Also included is what you need to look for in terms of the paperwork that must be done whenever you have radios repaired or installed.

WORK PILOTS/OWNERS ARE ALLOWED TO PERFORM

Unfortunately, when it comes to avionics, the FAA has pretty much left aircraft owners with little they can legally do to repair their own radios.

FAR Part 43, Appendix A details the categories of maintenance under which various repairs and alterations fall. There are two types of repair or alteration: major and minor. Major repairs and alterations must be signed off by IAs or by an authorized repair station (meaning that the repair station's certificate permits that specific repair or alteration). Minor repairs and alterations can be done by an Airframe and Powerplant Mechanic.

As the owner of the aircraft, you are allowed to perform preventive maintenance. Items that are considered preventive maintenance are listed at the end of Appendix A of FAR Part 43. And that list doesn't include one item of avionics-type repairs. In fact, the only mention of wiring at all is that you are permitted to repair landing light wiring. That's it.

So where does that leave you?

There is one legal way you can work on your aircraft. You can work on your aircraft as long as you are supervised by an appropriately licensed person. This person must directly supervise your work and sign it off in the logbooks.

An airframe mechanic is permitted to perform minor repairs on aircraft and their related appliances. This includes the avionics and all the wiring. An airframe mechanic is not permitted to perform major repairs on an appliance like a radio. An example of a major repair is calibration of a VOR head. This must be done either by an

IA or by an approved repair station. Basically, an airframe mechanic is limited to removal and installation of avionics, repairs to wiring, and inspection of installation for 100-hour inspections. A mechanic with the appropriate FCC license could repair transmitters as well.

It is important to realize that you are not even allowed to remove your #1 navcom. You cannot take your intercom out and bring it to an avionics shop for repair. It may sound ridiculous, but those are the rules, and you should be aware of them. You should also know that any time a mechanic removes, say, a transmitter for repair, the mechanic is required to log the removal and the subsequent reinstallation in the aircraft's logbooks. Hardly anyone does this, but FAR 43.9 mandates logging all maintenance, regardless of whether it's a major or minor repair or alteration, or preventive maintenance performed by the owner. Chapter 3 explains this more, as well as why record-keeping is so important.

To recap, if you want to work on your own avionics equipment, perhaps repair the broken wire on your push-to-talk switch or resolder that wire that is causing an intermittent problem on your mic jack, you need to do it under the supervision of at least an airframe mechanic, and it must be signed off in the logbooks by the mechanic. You'll also need a mechanic to supervise and sign off your removal and/or reinstallation of any piece of avionics.

3
Choosing avionics

THE DECISION TO BUY NEW RADIOS IS USUALLY DUE TO A REPETITIVE failure, an intermittent problem that never gets fixed, a noisy radio, or simply the desire to enter the modern age. Over 80 percent of aircraft built since the late 1960s have not had major radio modifications. If you end up with one of these airplanes, you'll no doubt see at least one ancient radio lurking in a well-worn instrument panel. Many of these old radios are tube-type and so tired they are ready to take a long vacation in a dark cabinet. While it may be possible to get these radios working, you have to wonder how long they'll continue to operate, and will they do so reliably? Ask yourself: will this old radio be a bottomless pit into which you'll be constantly throwing money?

One manufacturer, McCoy Avionics, offers a retrofit face for King KX170-series navcoms. The MAC 1700-series Control/Display unit replaces the usually worn-out mechanical frequency selectors in the King radio with a modern, digital-readout, multiple-memory front end. The upgrade kit costs from $1295 to $1495, plus the labor for installation (about $300). One problem to watch for, however, is the condition of the rest of the radio. What's the sense of spending that much money to upgrade a radio that is on its last legs? If you decide to go this route, I recommend you have your old nav-com bench checked first to determine if its components are operating at the proper levels. Also, any upgrades and modifications that are available should have been done, or should be done as part of the front-end replacement to ensure the radio will last for a reasonable amount of time.

Another low-cost approach is the simple removal of the old radio and replacement with a new radio that slides into the existing rack. Narco offers these slide-in replacements for older Cessna-made ARC radios, and TKM Michel Aviation Products makes slide-in replacements for older King, Narco, and ARC radios. In many cases, no modifications are necessary—just slide the new radio in and away you go. Even some of the older tube-type ARC radios can be replaced this way, although in some cases an adapter kit is necessary. This is a good way to upgrade your navcoms, except for the wiring, which can be a weak link in the whole system. The wiring could by itself be a source of noise and pesky intermittent problems that weren't so evident with the older radios because they were less sensitive than the new ones. If you suspect any kind of wiring problem, have it taken care of before spending money on new, slide-in replacement radios.

Trying to cut corners with avionics is like placing a time bomb in the instrument panel: there isn't any way you can know when electronic components will fail, but the odds of failure are greater when the radio already has two strikes against it. Using old radios with new front ends helps you operate the radio without mechanical frequency selection problems, but doesn't eliminate the possibility of electronic failure in the rest of the radio. And relying on existing wiring that may be several years old is further stacking the deck against safety and reliability.

If you have one of the following radios, it can be replaced by a slide-in unit offered by Narco or TKM Michel, offering fully modern capabilities that designers didn't even think of back in the 1960s. The new radios comply with the new 0.003-percent frequency-stability requirements, and most don't require any modifications for installation, but you'll need to check to be sure.

ARC (Aircraft Radio Corp., formerly owned by Cessna Aircraft Company, since sold to Sigma-Tek):

RT308B	RT508A
RT328A	RT517
RT329C	RT540
RT328D	RT514R
RT328T	RT515A-1
RT528A	RT385
RT528E	RT485

Bendix/King (takes McCoy digital front end or TKM Michel slide-in):

KX170 series   KX175 series

Narco:

Com 11	Com 111B
Com 11A	Com 120
Com 11B	Com 10
Com 111	Com 110

Besides maintenance and reliability problems, one of the reasons you might be considering replacing old equipment is simply all the new bells and whistles that come with new avionics. The other important reason is safety in the form of reliability and accuracy. If much of your business depends on the availability of your airplane, then you'll be sensitive to the need to have radios that are subject to minimum downtime and provide accurate, reliable service.

A clean, well-designed avionics installation in a Beech Bonanza A36 instrument panel.

USED RADIOS

Are you considering buying used radios? If so, your best bet might be to buy an entire package that was removed from another airplane, not a mixmash of miscellaneous boxes accumulated from several different airplanes. A system that functioned well as an integrated package has a greater potential of working reliably after being installed than a hodgepodge system and furthermore shouldn't be a warranty nightmare. The worst thing you can do is try to put together an avionics system consisting of various radios from different manufacturers. If you have to buy used radios, make sure they are all of one make. The reliability and savings in installation time will be more than worth any extra cost.

There are various precautions to watch for when considering buying used radios. Perhaps the previous owner had an intermittent problem with them and wanted to get rid of them. Have all the factory modifications been done to keep the radios up to date? Will you be allowed to return the radios if they don't pass testing at your avionics shop? Does the used radio have all the features you need?

With used avionics more than 10 years old, consider that parts might be difficult to obtain. Or they might be available, but at significantly high cost because of low availability. Do you have the time to wait for replacement parts to be shipped from an obscure source that hung on to all their old inventory?

The so-called "yellow tag" is a method used by repair stations to identify items that have been repaired and officially returned to service. The color yellow, despite what you may have heard, does not connote any special kind of status to the repaired or overhauled part. Yellow has simply been settled on as a convenient convention; the tag could be any color at all. An important consideration when buying used, yellow-tagged radios is that the FAA now requires that all documentation pertaining to a particular repair must accompany the repaired item. Most repair stations use yellow tags, and if you read the tag, you'll see a note that references a work-order number. For a repaired or overhauled radio to be legal, the actual work order must be attached that lists the parts used, what the technician did to the unit, and how it was tested after the repair. You'll find that this is rarely done, and you might have to insist, but do so. It's important that you know the pedigree of your avionics, and this knowledge will come in handy if you ever sell your airplane. If the yellow tag doesn't have a work order attached to it, don't buy the unit, no matter how good the price.

DETECTING STOLEN RADIOS

Beware of stolen radios. Expensive products always bring the unscrupulous out of the woodwork.

One way to check for stolen items is to check serial numbers against the stolen-radio listing compiled by the Aviation Crime Prevention Institute (ACPI). Most radio shops subscribe to this list, so they should be able to provide one to you.

Radio thieves have a few tricks up their sleeves, however, and you need to be watchful of these tricks, both as an owner and potential avionics buyer. Their cleverest trick results in a set of stolen radios that no one ever suspects is stolen. Here's how it works: They fly into a dark, unattended airport in the middle of the night. They have previously checked out the airport and pinpointed the airplanes they are going to rob. The robbers open the door on the first airplane, say it has a full panel of King digital-display avionics. Opening the door is simple, by the way. Airplane locks are incredibly cheap, and a set of about fifty keys will open most door locks on most airplanes at any airport. They remove all the panel-mounted avionics using a hex-key wrench. This takes about three minutes. They leave the door unlocked.

At airplane number two, which has the exact same radios, the robbers unlock the door and remove all of its radios. Then they install the radios taken from airplane number one into the panel of airplane number two, and lock its door after carefully removing any traces of their illegal entry.

The robbers take off. The total time for the switch is about ten to fifteen minutes, max. Next morning, the owner of airplane number one gets a big surprise: all the radios are gone. Naturally, the owner files a report with the police and insurance company. Being conscientious, the owner has a record of the stolen radios' serial numbers.

The owner of airplane number two never notices he is flying with a new set of radios, unless he has a reason at some later date to note serial numbers and compare them with those of his original radios. Perhaps he or she will think the avionics shop mixed them up.

Eventually the serial numbers for airplane number one's stolen radios get on the ACPI list. Yet those radios will probably never be found because they are sitting in airplane number two's instrument panel. And someday an airplane owner trying to save some money will end up owning the radios that were stolen out of airplane number two's panel because those serial numbers are still "legit." Pretty clever, huh?

Are stolen radios that big of a problem? The ACPI reports that 158 pieces of avionics were stolen in 1992. This figure has dropped for the fifth straight year, so fewer radios *are* being stolen, but, if you can afford to, buy new radios.

ANTITHEFT STRATEGIES

Airplanes are so easy to break into, it's pitiful. Plus, many airports can't afford night security, so what are you supposed to do to protect that $15,000 instrument panel? The best solution (and the most expensive) is to keep your airplane hangared. This isn't always possible, especially when away from home base, but there are other options.

Because airplane locks are so easy to open, the first line of defense is to install a better lock. Barrel-type tubular key locks are available that fit most light airplanes. The easiest way to replace the lock and find one that fits is to remove the old lock and take it to a locksmith so you can be sure of getting the correct size. Remember that you'll have to do this under your mechanic's supervision to make it legal. A barrel lock on a Piper Cherokee cabin door and baggage compartment will make the airplane very difficult to break into unless the robber chooses to break the windshield. Curiously, many airplane robberies result in little or no airframe damage, perhaps because the robbers are also pilots and have some modicum of respect for airplanes.

You can install barrel locks on Cessna singles, but why bother? The side windows on Cessna singles are easy to open, so having a door lock is sort of silly. In many cases, all you need to do to open a locked Cessna door is to simply rock the wings: the pilot's door, if not adjusted for a very tight fit, will pop right open.

First off, keep all windows covered with sunshields at all times when not flying. This will keep people from admiring your instrument panels and the goodies therein.

Second, consider buying one of those thick, metal instrument-panel covers that lock in place when you're done flying. You'd need some special tools to get one of these off, and most robbers want to get in and out quickly so they won't take the time to deal with a good panel cover. The other benefit of these covers is that they prevent people from seeing what's in the panel in the first place. Don't install a car alarm. It would be a paperwork nightmare to start with, plus any kind of wind will set it off.

Here's another scenario that will make your wallet lighter. You signed the bill of sale, the airplane is yours, and you fly it home. Everything checked out okay on your test flight except for a few minor items that the owner agreed to have fixed before you picked up the airplane. Surprise! On the way home, the avionics take a dump. What happened?

The seller pulled a switch, replacing the radios that were in the airplane during the test flight with defective or older models. It's hard to believe, but I've seen it happen, and it probably will happen again. In this particular case, the buyer hired an attorney and was able to recover damages, but how about you? Will you check close enough before you pay for the airplane?

NEW RADIOS

Rather than installing "experienced" equipment, check the costs of a new avionics package. You'll enjoy a new warranty, sometimes as much as two to three years depending on the manufacturer, and all the features you'd expect from modern avionics.

Regardless of the equipment you select, your choice should be guided by determining what will give you long-term reliability. This includes not only the avionics itself, but also the shop that installs it. In other words, does the shop stock and provide loaners for the types of radios you're thinking of buying? How long will the shop provide warranty for its installation, and what is covered by its installation warranty? You may pay less for a particular radio, but to what purpose if its subcomponents are subject to frequent failure or if the shop sells it so cheaply it can't afford to support you after the sale.

It's important to find out the terms for warranty repairs before spending thousands of dollars on new radios. You might be interested in knowing, for instance, that Narco Avionics no longer sells parts for current production radios (and some older radios that use the same parts) to its dealers. Narco wants the dealer who sold you the radio to send it back to Narco for repair, and Narco says its turn-around time is three days.

Another major benefit of replacing old avionics with modern equipment is that the new installation can free up a lot of instrument panel space. You might find that in considering a new package, you can add a piece of equipment like loran or GPS where there wasn't room before.

There are many advantages to installing new equipment, but there are still potential problems. Planning and good communication with the avionics shop manager during the negotiation stages will reduce the obstacles you are bound to encounter.

A good stereo system can make long flights more enjoyable. The installer created a new over-lay on the right side to support the additional weight of the stereo, intercom, clock, and RMI.

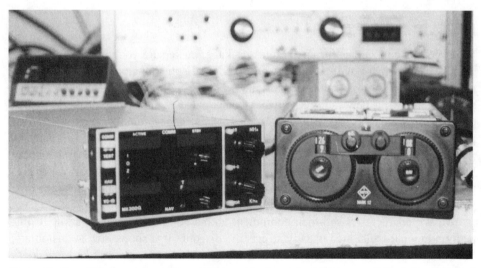

Out with the old tube-style radios, and in with the new solid-state, digital-display, and more reliable avionics.

VISITING AN AVIONICS SHOP

When visiting an avionics shop for the first time to discuss costs and quotes, get satisfactory answers to the following questions before going any further.

Can the manager show you examples of their installation work? Actual airplanes are preferable, but some shops keep a photo album of their custom installations.

Is the shop a qualified dealer for the type of avionics you are considering buying? Dealers are authorized to perform warranty work on your radios, can usually get parts quicker, and can sometimes even get factory loaners for you. A dealer will also sell you the latest version of a particular radio, not last year's unsold leftovers, unless you ask for them specifically.

Is the shop a repair station or a nonapproved shop? If it is a repair station, does the repair station license permit the type of work you are considering having done? If nonapproved, are the personnel licensed and experienced for the job you are paying for?

Ask for the grand tour of the facility. While you might not know what to look for, the shop should have all necessary test equipment for testing and repairing the type of avionics it sells. Are the people working there friendly and willing to answer questions? Does management send employees out for training on a regular basis? Does the shop appear organized, or is there trash all over the place? Are incoming defective radios tagged and properly stored in an organized fashion, or are they just haphazardly lying around? While some good shops can appear disorganized, signs of sloppiness can warn of sloppy quality. If you feel the shop manager is rushing you through the tour and not taking the time to explain what the shop has to offer, how long it has been in business, and the shop's philosophy and quality standards, find a shop where you're more comfortable with the management.

INSTALLATION COST

When getting cost quotes for an avionics package, make sure you understand exactly what is included. You will probably want to comparison shop, and this is impossible unless you know that one quote, for instance, includes indirect costs such as antennas, switches, relays, a new radome, circuit-breaker wiring, improved speakers, microphone and headphone jacks, new instrument panel shock mounts, new instrument panel, and reupholstered glareshield.

Some quotes may include these costs in the total package price, while others may break the costs down. The important thing is to make sure you know what you're getting for a particular package price. For more accurate comparison-shopping purposes, you'd be better off asking for complete breakdowns of all costs.

Most manufacturers sell their equipment with a 30- to 40-percent markup. Competition in a particular area usually affects the discount that shops give to customers, but don't forget, if the shop doesn't make enough on the sale, it won't be in business for too long. A 15-percent discount is the going rate in most areas, but this depends on how much of the installation cost is included or if the installation charge is extra.

If you bring your own radios that you have purchased elsewhere, expect to pay a reasonable shop rate for installation. Some shops break even on the installation charge and make their money on the sale of the radios. If this is the case, don't expect the installation charge for radios that you bring to be the same as the installation charge for your buddy who bought his radios from that shop. Also expect that the shop will want to fully test the radios that you bring.

You have the right to expect the avionics shop to advise you of the best avionics package for your airplane and your budget. Although you might not be able to spend all you'd like at this point, there are options. For example, you can have all the equipment racks and wiring for an entire package installed with, say, one navcom and a transponder. Later, as the money becomes available, you can fill up the empty racks one by one until your avionics system is complete. This requires some planning on your part to give you an operational system to start with, less the additional equipment to be added later. If you're planning to purchase RNAV later, for example, it may be necessary to install an adapter temporarily because the #1 nav circuitry works through the RNAV. If your plans call for installation of GPS later on, then you might forego even considering RNAV at this point. Possibly by the time you buy your GPS unit, they will be approved for IFR navigation anyway.

MAIL-ORDER PURCHASES

Some people have pretty good luck with mail order. The mail-order companies must be doing fairly well because the companies seem to keep growing. As an avionics manager, I did some extensive work with mail-order outlets, and each was pretty good to work with. If any item failed to perform as advertised, they made good on it. Note that these items were mostly headsets and microphones. It's your decision, but if mail order is the choice you make, deal with well-known and established companies.

The thing that bothers me about mail order is the lack of support for repair, installation, and training. You might save a few dollars ordering by mail, but in the long run, those savings could haunt you when you least expect it. It's a lot harder to get support from a company halfway across the country.

It's important to find out if the unit you're getting from a mail order company is the latest, with all the up-to-date modifications incorporated by the factory. Or will you need to pay to add these mods, then have the unit tested? When comparison shopping, avionics dealers should give you a price that is for the latest version, complete with warranty. Many shops don't like customers to bring in their own avionics, and you can expect to pay more for installation if you do so.

Remember that with mail order, you pay the shipping for any defective merchandise. If you receive something that might be defective, you could end up having to pay your local avionics shop to test it. Having not bought it from the local shop, you might experience a longer turn-around time because the shop has a responsibility to meet its immediate customer needs before any headache repairs like yours where the prospects of you spending much money at the shop aren't very good.

I like a good deal as well as the next person, but I'm not enamored of the mail-order business. I think that mail order is a risky hobby when dealing in aviation radios. If you're lucky and everything works, you're in good shape. But when you consider the problems that normally come as part of any avionics package, do you want to take on the additional hassle of having to deal with long-distance suppliers?

OTHER PURCHASING CONSIDERATIONS

Deciding what brand to buy is a personal decision. You may be guided by advice from other owners, or by doing research on your own. Before you get close to deciding, you might want to start reading some of the avionics magazines listed at the end of this book. Also, *The Aviation Consumer* magazine has done extensive reader surveys of avionics reliability. You might try to get hold of those back issues to help in your decision.

Technical standard order (TSO) requirements

Avionics that have met TSO requirements, which are just a set of minimum standards, must be used in aircraft flown for commercial purposes, such as charter and airlines. As an owner flying under FAR Part 91 or for an aircraft used for flight instruction or rental, TSOed radios are not required. Non-TSOed radios are usually less expensive and perform just as well. TSOed radios may add more resale value to your airplane, especially if it is a light twin that might be used someday for charter. But there is no requirement for you to use TSOed radios.

Build-it-yourself radios

For those of you who used to drool over the Heathkit catalog, Radio Systems Technology (RST) offers some inexpensive avionics kits that you can build. The company makes audio panels, intercoms, marker beacon receivers, and headsets in both kit- and factory-built versions. Later in 1993, RST will be offering com and nav radios as well. RST also offers parts for builders of composite kits to make their own concealed antennas, and they sell an *Antenna Reference Text* that discusses how to build the antennas. See the Suppliers section at the end of this book for the company's phone number and address.

Cooling fans

Avionics cooling fans are essential with today's jam-packed electronics. Even though modern radios don't contain tubes anymore, to get the fantastic capabilities out of these new radios, circuit boards are densely packed with heat-generating components. For proper operation and long life, it's crucial to get cooling air flowing through the radio stacks to dissipate heat.

Ambient-air temperatures can adversely affect avionics equipment, severely limiting service life, even when not turned on. Congestion behind the panel, inadequate venting through the glare shield, and the greenhouse effect of an unprotected airplane sitting outside without windshield covers all contribute to reduced avionics life.

This is one way of adding a cooling fan to just one new black box. Most avionics manufacturers will consider warranties void if radios are not properly cooled.

Any temperature buildup beyond the recommended operating range (the maximum is 131 degrees F for TSOed radios) will begin the destructive cycle. For each 18-degree rise in temperature, the life of solid-state circuitry is reduced by 50 percent. Although the radio might continue to operate, failure could occur during a later heat wave without warning or become intermittent because of a component that weakened from excess heat.

In older radios, recurring failures can be due to heat-sensitive components. Wax-filled capacitors used in some old radios, for instance, spill out their innards when subjected to intensive heat behind the instrument panel. Normal operation levels deteriorate as components grow old, their insulation dries out and cracks, and higher voltages sneak out through these escape routes. One repair might get the radio going again, but then a domino effect takes place. The new, stronger component is installed, and the weaker older components in the same circuit absorb the new load allowed by the new component, and finally another part dies. This process can continue for months, and at some point a smart avionics technician will simply suggest replacing one of these radios with a new one, rather than replace all the components one at a time.

Some installers connect a cooling air hose from a scoop on the outside of the airplane to the radio stack. While that is better than nothing, a better solution is to install an avionics cooling fan that runs any time the master switch is on.

If you are having new radios installed, make sure the radio stack has room for a cooling air plenum. A *plenum* is a plastic chamber that attaches to the radio rack and directs cooling air onto each radio in the rack. Hoses from the cooling fan can be attached to the plenum.

The cost of a cooling fan is much less than the repair bill for heat-damaged radios and is worth it in terms of the reliability of the equipment. To provide adequate airflow, at least 0.002-inch spacing should be left between radios stacked on top of each other.

4
Installation

WHILE YOU WON'T BE DIRECTLY INVOLVED IN THE INSTALLATION UNLESS you are building your own airplane, you should discuss the following points with your avionics shop manager to be sure they are taken into consideration during your installation. These factors will go a long way towards increasing the reliability and maintainability of your installation. If you are building your own airplane, use these points as guidelines for your avionics installation.

One of the most important factors to consider during an installation is designing the installation for maintainability. When access is easy, technicians are more likely to perform quality repairs. But when a technician must battle for hours just to reach the problem area, their decision-making ability could be strained and dampened with sweat. Besides the effort in accessing the avionics, damage to surrounding wiring and connectors could occur without the technician's knowledge. Fixing one problem and creating another doesn't help you, the owner. From the outset, then, design for maintainability is a worthwhile goal.

The second goal, and one that is also important, is design for reliability. This involves work of high quality to prevent problems caused by vibration, moisture, chafing, RF interference, and other sources of trouble.

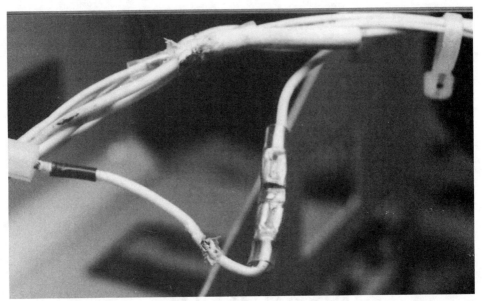

An excellent example of poor wiring installation. This airplane's instrument panel lights kept popping the circuit breaker. The pilot found these chafing wires after removing the radar from its rack.

The initial part of the installation will involve building wiring harnesses, then roughly routing the harness in the airplane to see how it will fit. During the rough routing, the installer should note all points that will require special attention to avoid chafing and RF interference. As the actual routing takes place, the installer will take care of those potential trouble spots by installing clamps, protecting the harness with plastic spiral wrap, installing caterpillar grommets in lightning holes, and avoiding RF interference by properly routing cables that could interfere with each other electronically.

To prevent chafing, all wiring harnesses, plumbing, and installed equipment should not come into hard contact with the structure or with each other. At no time should equipment or equipment racks come into direct contact with nearby structure. Establish at least a quarter inch or more for adequate clearance, because skins and structure can flex during flight.

If the wiring harness is laying gently on smooth aluminum skin with no sharp edges, the likelihood of damaged wiring is slim. The key is relative motion and pressure. The greater the pressure and relative motion, the greater the potential for insulation breakdown. To be safe, it's preferable to clamp the harness to protect it from rubbing against the skin.

Shock-mounted equipment racks must take into account the movement of the radio during normal aircraft operations. The same is true of wiring harness clearance from plumbing lines, especially those carrying oil, fuel, and oxygen; there should be no physical contact between adjoining plumbing, wiring, or structure. Never use plumbing for primary support. It's okay to use standoffs to separate harnesses from

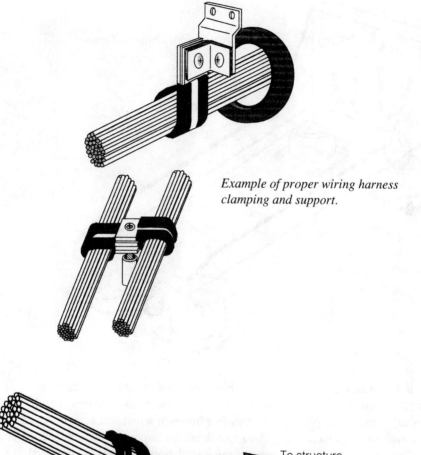

*Example of proper wiring harness
clamping and support.*

To structure

*One way of spacing a wiring
harness away from the aircraft
structure, to prevent chafing.*

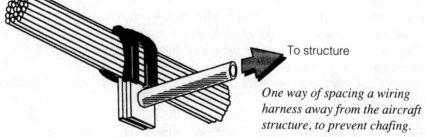

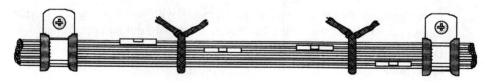

Wiring harnesses should be supported every 15 inches.

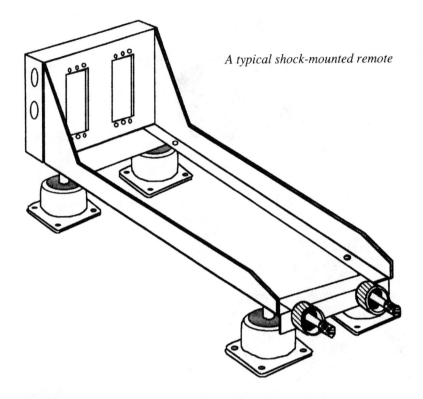

A typical shock-mounted remote

plumbing, but at no time should the plumbing carry the weight of the harness.

Wires are insulated, but the insulation isn't impervious to damage from sharp edges, heat, or excessive pressure such as that imposed when wires are clamped with nylon ties against a metal surface. For more detail on important harness-routing considerations to avoid RF interference, see the installation tips section contained in the chapter on that particular piece of equipment.

Designers must work to a consistent standard for harness installations that takes into account all these factors, plus what I call the "five don'ts":

- Don't limit clamping provisions. A sufficient quantity of clamps is necessary to prevent harness droop between clamps.

- Don't route harness to come into contact with sharp surfaces or ride against any moveable surface. Provide antichafing if necessary.

- Don't design location and space requirements without allowing for service loops (slack harness that will allow maintenance without harness damage).

- Don't design harnesses to route in hot areas without adequate thermal protection.

- Don't route harnesses in areas that are subject to chemical damage without protective conduit, such as landing gear wells and engine compartments.

MOUNTING BLACK BOXES

Follow these rules on mounting radio receivers, transmitters, amplifiers, and computers.

- Hard-mounted equipment can be installed as close as necessary to other equipment except for clearance needed for cooling (usually ¼ inch). Rack-to-equipment contact should take bonding into consideration with tension contacts and paint removal from the radio so that the tension contact is touching bare metal.

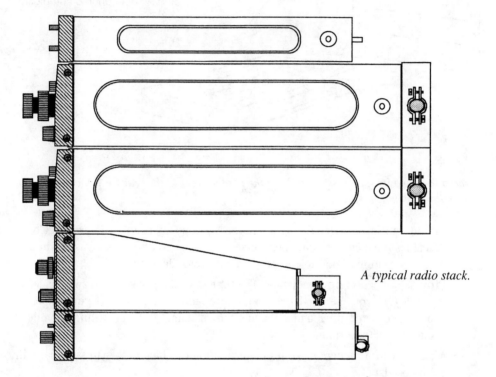

A typical radio stack.

- Provide harness supports at the back of the rack to alleviate stress on wiring and connectors that could cause difficult-to-troubleshoot failures down the line.
- Allow sufficient distance between the radio and the aircraft's skin. Normal airflow and aerodynamic stresses on the skin can cause changes in this clearance. The goal is to avoid any contact between the skin and the radio.
- Fasteners for holding radio racks in place should be secured with locking devices (either a lockwasher or locknut) to prevent vibration from allowing screws to loosen. This is especially important where radio racks sit above flight controls. If a loose radio rack could impinge on flight controls, it is a good idea to add supports to the rack as a backup to prevent flight control interference.

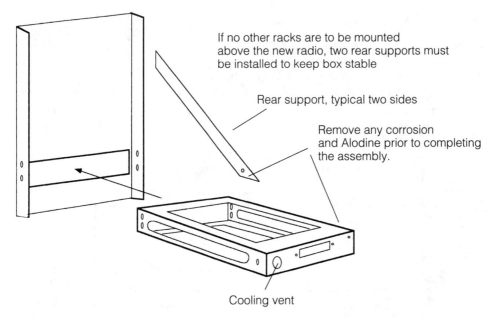

If no other racks are to be mounted above the new radio, two rear supports must be installed to keep box stable

Rear support, typical two sides

Remove any corrosion and Alodine prior to completing the assembly.

Cooling vent

A radio rack and its support system. Note the cooling vent at the rear for attachment to the cooling plenum.

- Provide sufficient space for wiring harness and coaxial cable connectors. Coaxial cables must enter the mating connector on the equipment in as straight and natural a routing as possible to prevent connector damage.

- Provide protection from moisture. The time to find out your windshield is leaking is *before* you spend $10,000 on a new radio installation. If you suspect a leak, spend some time under the instrument panel with a flashlight while a friend sprays the airplane with water.

- Make sure all fasteners used in the installation can handle the stresses that will be imposed.

- If the installation is in a pressurized aircraft, all areas that penetrate the pressure vessel must be sealed to prevent cabin pressure leakage. One small leak might not affect pressurization, but a number of small leaks could cause a significant drop in the ability to pressurize the cabin.

ANTENNAS

For specific information on antenna-mounting considerations, see chapter 7 and the chapters on the applicable equipment.

Antennas should always be mounted so they can be removed by one person from the outside of the aircraft. Costs of maintenance will be much higher if someone has to wriggle their way into the depths of the fuselage to hold nuts while someone turns a screwdriver to remove an antenna. Use blind fasteners like nutplates during installation to prevent this problem. This is especially important where the antenna mount point is covered by upholstery in the cockpit.

The coaxial cables and their mounting should be designed to allow antennas to be removed from the outside of the fuselage and pulled away from the skin at least two inches. Cable clamping should be snug but not restrictive, enough to secure the cable against excessive movement but still allow it to yield to the technician's coaxing during antenna troubleshooting or replacement.

OTHER INSTALLATION GUIDELINES

There are two primary sources of installation information your avionics shop should be using as technical references for avionics installations. The first is the avionics manufacturers' data, which includes information pertinent to its products. If you are interested, ask to see this data and confirm that your avionics installer is using it as a reference.

The second is broader in scope, but very useful, and that is the FAA's AC43.13-1A and 13-2A. This advisory circular, which is really a book, is entitled "Aircraft Inspection, Repair & Alterations" and gives detailed information on avionics installations and the structural alterations that must be done to accommodate new radios. There is even an entire chapter on antenna installations, and it includes plenty of information about wiring and electrical guidelines. For all the information it contains, AC43.13 is a bargain and is available from most aviation book distributors, pilot supply stores, and many FBOs.

PLACARDING

Placarding the instrument panel is the final step and can make the difference between a mediocre-looking or quality installation. Whether installing an entire suite of avionics or a new DME selector switch, it is imperative to identify the switches, lights, and circuit breakers that are an integral part of the installation.

Over the last 20 years, several methods have been used to make placards for instrument panels. The most accepted method, used by factories in their avionics installations, is silk-screening. This is where silk-screen ink is squeeged onto the panel though a silk-screen template, and it makes for a professional-looking, nearly flawless label. This is also the most expensive and time-consuming process.

Another approach is rub-on wax letters, but these wear off easily after exposure to normal use and sunlight. Sometimes applying clear lacquer on top of the wax letters makes them last longer, but it looks ugly and cheap when not done carefully. Engraving usually looks good, but one little mistake and the whole job has to be done over again, which takes time and more money.

One simple solution is a sticky-backed film that comes in clear or white and that can be placed in a copier or laser printer to create instant placards. This is manufactured by Hawk Corporation (see Appendix B). The only drawback is that the lettering is black-on-white or black-on-clear, unless you use a color printer or copier. Plus you'll need a computer program to create the placards.

The simplest, quickest, and easiest way to create custom placards is using a Kroy or Brother labeling machine. These are available fairly inexpensively from any office-supply store and have a variety of features that makes them ideal for custom placarding, including vertical lettering, various type (letter) sizes, and an assortment of colors. The lettering obtained from these machines is not only waterproof but it's highly resistant to abrasion and fading from ultraviolet light. The actual lettering is on the opposite side from the exposed surface and is virtually impervious to damage. I took a razor blade and scraped it through the vinyl surface without exposing the lettering. The surface is such that the installer can remove the glossy finish with a 3M Scotchbrite pad or 400-grit sandpaper, leaving a flat finish. With the heavy traffic of pilots' hands rubbing across instrument panels and the damaging effects of sunlight, placards are subject to a lot of wear and tear. The labels produced by these units show every indication they can handle the job.

Applying placards

Applying placards properly is an art. The goal is satisfactory appearance and long-term endurance. The following installation discussion describes creating a placard with the Brother labeler.

When dealing with a smooth surface, first simply clean with a mild soap-and-water solution. Using alcohol or other solvents could remove old paint, change its color, or make the cleaned area glossier than the rest of the instrument panel. The soap-and-water mixture is less apt to cause this kind of problem. Rinse with clean water or a clean wet cloth before installing the placard, and allow to dry.

After cutting and removing the placard from the labeler, cut off excess material as close as possible to the letters with a sharp razor blade. With the tip of your cutting tool, lift the letters from the backing material. When removing the backing and handling the placard, do not touch the adhesive; the oils in your fingers will prevent permanent adhesion to the desired surface. Hold the placard using the razor blade, and bringing the placard into position, let one corner of it touch the panel, allowing the adhesive to grab. Adjust the other end so it's straight, then press firmly on the placard with a finger to seal it in place.

On large placards, use the discarded backing to rub the placard to remove air bubbles. If there are any bubbles left, use a sharp needle to prick the bubbles then rub the placard to push the trapped air through the pinhole.

A textured surface is a little more complicated, but can accept placards with a little additional effort. On some lightly textured surfaces such as painted panels, gently rub the area with an ink eraser to smooth out the majority of ridges and valleys, allowing the placard to seat firmly on the panel. If the surface is plastic, such as a pedestal or sidewall or plastic false instrument panel, a small amount of lacquer thinner dabbed on the end of a sharpened but slightly blunted ink eraser will smooth the plastic. Be careful not to smooth out beyond the area that will be covered by the placard. Once dry, install the placard.

If you're concerned about the placard's edges lifting from heat or wear and tear, gently apply a thin coat of flat clear lacquer (not lacquer thinner) on the top of the placard and carefully around the edges. To get some lacquer from a spray can, simply spray a small amount into the cap of the spray can and allow it to evaporate a little because it is easier to handle when slightly thicker. The discarded backing tape serves quite well to transfer a thin quantity of clear lacquer to the edges of the placard. The sharp edge of the placard will wick the thin lacquer along its perimeter. Allow the lacquer to dry thoroughly before touching the placard.

Vinyl surfaces such as those used on Beechcraft panels are nothing more than an industrial vinyl contact paper. This is a petroleum-based product that may excrete an oil film that will resist the adhesion of the placard. Simply clean the intended location with soap and water or alcohol, let dry, and apply the placard.

One other use for the labeler is to make placards for annunciator lights, circuit breakers, and for wire identification. To make a wire placard, simply print out the desired number twice, leaving a quarter inch between the two numbers. Then remove the backing and wrap the label around the wire and stick the two free ends to each other, leaving a clearly tagged wire, which will do wonders for making maintenance easier. Yet another use is to identify terminal blocks, Cannon plugs, and other connectors.

PAPERWORK FOR INSTALLATIONS AND REPAIRS

You've probably heard this before, but the job isn't done until the paperwork is done. The paperwork attending an avionics installation is considerable. The items you should expect and make sure you end up with after the job is done include: logbooks, FAA Form 337, weight-and-balance and equipment list updates, and an accurate invoice.

Logbook

1. Keep a complete, detailed, legible logbook entry listing exactly what was installed, the serial numbers of all radios installed, the details on how the work was accomplished, and a reference that an FAA Form 337 was completed and the weight-and-balance and equipment list was updated.

2. After you agree to the installation but before the actual radios are installed, make a note of all serial numbers on the equipment you are buying. The best place to make this note is in your aircraft logbook, next to the page where the shop will log the installation, or in a separate avionics log. This will make it easier to determine if your radios have been stolen and will increase the value of your airplane by showing prospective buyers that you are a stickler for organized, accurate records.

3. This also applies to repairs. Remember that FAR Part 43 requires that any maintenance be recorded in the aircraft records. Lots of people are in the habit of removing a radio, taking it to the avionics shop, then reinstalling it without making any logbook entry. Without a record of what's been done, how will you be able to troubleshoot a recurring problem? Or what if the avionics shop has already replaced the capacitor twice and the transponder still doesn't work? You could rely on your memory, or you could insist on logbook entries.

4. Always bring your logbook with you to the avionics shop and ask for a detailed entry to go along with any repair. You can use a separate avionics log if you want. This will help considerably when you run into recurring intermittent problems and can increase the resale value of your airplane. If you don't have your logbook with you when you get something repaired, ask for a typed label that you can place into the log when you get home.

FAA Form 337

An FAA Form 337 must be filled out. At least two copies are required, one for the owner, and one to be sent to the local FAA office within 48 hours. A Form 337 is required whenever a major alteration is made to an aircraft, and any avionics installation should be considered to be a major alteration. Some repair stations might suggest that they aren't required to fill out a 337; however, FAR Part 43 allows repair stations to forego the 337 only for major repairs, not for major alterations. Most FAA inspectors concur that any avionics installation, including a mere intercom installation, is a major alteration and calls for a 337 to be completed. The shop might want to keep a copy for its records.

Weight-and-balance and equipment list update

No matter what you've heard, there is no rule or advisory circular stating that items that weigh less than one pound can be ignored for weight-and-balance purposes. If that was true, then how many under-one-pound items would have to be installed before you'd have to start adding them up and noting their effect on the center of gravity and empty weight of the airplane?

Every item added needs to be accounted for including lightweight intercoms, wiring, connectors, etc. All items and their weights need to be listed on the equipment list. Shops that take pride in their work will produce a neatly typed or word-processed weight-and-balance and equipment list update for your records.

Don't accept delivery of your airplane without this paperwork. It really doesn't take that long to accomplish and is essential for the legal status of your airplane. The airplane is not legal to fly until the paperwork is completed—it's that simple.

		Form Approved OMB No. 2120-0020

US Department of Transportation
Federal Aviation Administration

MAJOR REPAIR AND ALTERATION
(Airframe, Powerplant, Propeller, or Appliance)

Form Approved OMB No. 2120-0020
For FAA Use Only
Office Identification

INSTRUCTIONS: Print or type all entries. See FAR 43.9, FAR 43 Appendix B, and AC 43.9-1 (or subsequent revision thereof) for instructions and disposition of this form. This report is required by law (49 U.S.C. 1421). Failure to report can result in a civil penalty not to exceed $1,000 for each such violation (Section 901 Federal Aviation Act of 1958).

1. Aircraft	Make		Model	
	Serial No.		Nationality and Registration Mark	

2. Owner	Name *(As shown on registration certificate)*	Address *(As shown on registration certificate)*

3. For FAA Use Only

	4. Unit Identification			5. Type	
Unit	Make	Model	Serial No.	Repair	Alteration
AIRFRAME	~~~~~~~~~~~~~~~~~(As described in Item 1 above)~~~~~~~~~~~~~~~~				
POWERPLANT					
PROPELLER					
APPLIANCE	Type				
	Manufacturer				

6. Conformity Statement

A. Agency's Name and Address	B. Kind of Agency	C. Certificate No.
	U.S. Certificated Mechanic	
	Foreign Certificated Mechanic	
	Certificated Repair Station	
	Manufacturer	

D. I certify that the repair and/or alteration made to the unit(s) identified in item 4 above and described on the reverse or attachments hereto have been made in accordance with the requirements of Part 43 of the U.S. Federal Aviation Regulations and that the information furnished herein is true and correct to the best of my knowledge.

Date	Signature of Authorized Individual

7. Approval for Return To Service

Pursuant to the authority given persons specified below, the unit identified in item 4 was inspected in the manner prescribed by the Administrator of the Federal Aviation Administration and is ☐ APPROVED ☐ REJECTED

BY	FAA Flt. Standards Inspector	Manufacturer	Inspection Authorization	Other *(Specify)*
	FAA Designee	Repair Station	Person Approved by Transport Canada Airworthiness Group	
Date of Approval or Rejection	Certificate or Designation No.	Signature of Authorized Individual		

FAA Form 337, used to document major repair or alteration. This is the first page of the double-sided form. The back page is used to describe the work performed.

INSTALLATION CHECKLIST

Use this checklist as a guide to help you through the avionics installation. You might want to go over this with your avionics shop manager before beginning the process to see if you both agree that these are important points to cover.

The checklist is split into three phases. The first phase is for before any work begins, the second is for about halfway through the job (while the guts of your airplane are fully exposed), and the third is upon completion of the job.

Phase 1

- Meet with the avionics manager, tour the shop, look at examples of work, and contact customers who have had work done by the shop.
- Finish researching and decide on the equipment you want.
- Discuss the cost of equipment and installation with the shops you're considering. Get firm written quotes with as much breakdown as possible of the avionics equipment, labor, and miscellaneous parts (such as antennas, wiring, placards, etc.). Discuss what to do if the installers discover unrelated defects while they have the airplane opened up.
- After choosing a shop to do the work, get a time commitment. Discuss possible penalties for delays in completing work in the allotted time frame.
- Along with a firm dollar and time quote, ask for a sketch of the planned panel layout, harness routing, and antenna locations.
- Find out if major wiring harness changes will be needed. Will the shop construct its own harness using mil-spec high-temperature wire or use the harness provided by some avionics manufacturers?
- What type of clamping of wiring harness will be used, especially over flight controls?
- How will bare metal be corrosion-proofed?
- Will the shop do all placarding? What type of placarding? Will it guarantee appearance of placarding?
- Verify that everything works, or note what doesn't, before bringing the airplane in for the installation so you know whether or not something might have been the result of the installation.
- Assure that the shop will provide wiring schematics and assembly notes after the job is done. If the shop is building your wiring harness, a schematic will be needed for anyone to work on the system later on.
- Will existing avionics and static/altimeter system be tested while the airplane is opened up?
- Take both close-up and overall photos of the interior and exterior of the airplane and the instrument panel before the job begins.

Phase 2

- Verify that all harnesses are being clamped adequately.

- Are harnesses clearing control cables and the control column?

- Have the installers discovered any defects while digging around in your airplane's innards? Will these defects be taken care of? Who will do the work and how much will it cost?

- Look inside the belly, through the inspection panels that have been opened up in the floor. Is there trash in there that should be removed? Ask if you can do this to save some money and keep your airplane clean.

- Have all drill shavings, aluminum cuttings, rivets, dropped nuts and screws, etc. been removed prior to reassembly?

- Confirm that any commitment to use high-quality Mil-spec wiring is being upheld.

- Ask to look at all opened up areas. Look for anything out of place or obvious defects. Ask questions based on what you learn from reading this book.

Phase 3

- Ask for documentation of static/altimeter/transponder tests if they were done during the installation.

- Ask for documentation of testing of all systems after completion of installation. Better yet, ask if you can be there during testing.

- Test-fly the airplane with the shop manager and note any discrepancies that need to be taken care of and that are the responsibility of the avionics shop.

- Has all required paperwork been completed?
  ~ Has aircraft logbook been signed, with proper dates and tach times noted and an accurate description of the work that was done?
  ~ Is there a listing of new avionics and their serial numbers in aircraft log or radio log?
  ~ Has FAA Form 337 been filled out? One copy goes to the owner, and one goes to the FAA (within 48 hours). Most shops also keep a copy for their records, although it isn't required by law.
  ~ Are weight-and-balance data and equipment list updates complete? Regardless of what you have heard, there is no "less-than-a-pound" exclusion. If some new equipment has been added, its weight, datum, and effect on the CG must be noted.

- Take "after" photos and compare with "before" photos. This reduces the likelihood of differing opinions on prior damage or damage that happened during the installation. It also ensures there is nothing missing or changed compared to the way the airplane was when you brought it in for the work.

INSTALLATION

It is extremely important that all paperwork be done before you take delivery. Do not accept an excuse that the shop is too busy and that the paperwork will be filled out later. It is a legal fact that the job is not done until the paperwork is completed, regardless of whether or not the paperwork makes the airplane safe to fly. When you leave the shop, the paperwork goes with you, in exchange for the check that could lighten your wallet considerably.

5
Microphones, headsets, intercoms, and speakers

Microphones, headsets, intercoms, and speakers are also the basic devices through which you interface with your communications radios and happen to be a source of a majority of the problems you'll encounter.

THE MICROPHONE

A microphone must deliver your voice clearly during reception and transmission. Because the microphone must survive heat and cold, high humidity or dryness, excessive vibration, and rough handling, durability and reliability are essential. If you're buying a new microphone, ask around to see what other pilots are using. While low cost and low weight might appeal to you, find those pilots who have microphones that are over a year old and are still operating reliably. Only well-designed, sturdily built units will sustain the rough environment of being thrown around an airplane trip after trip.

There are three basic types of aircraft microphones: carbon, dynamic, and electret. Each type can be made into the noise-canceling type, although the noise-canceling is better with dynamic and electret mics.

Microphone plug. There are three active sections: tip (key line), mic (modulation, or your voice signals), and sleeve (common ground). Periodically clean plugs with a 3M Scotchbrite pad until shiny.

Cracks in cord indicate potential failure points.

Carbon microphone

The carbon mic has been around for a long time and is the simplest and least expensive of the three types. You might have used one like the familiar square black Telex 66C.

Telex 66C carbon microphone.

In a carbon mic, a diaphragm is attached to a small chamber containing densely packed carbon granules. As the sound waves from your voice strike the diaphragm, the carbon granules are compressed. The compressed carbon particles alter an electrical current that is being applied across the carbon chamber. The changes in the electrical current are amplified within the com radio, then transmitted.

Drawbacks of the carbon mic include inherent noise, only fair frequency response, plus the carbon granules become more tightly packed; they stick together as they age, causing unwanted signals and reduced capacity. You might have seen a pilot whacking their carbon mic on the dashboard, and this is a valid technique because it loosens up the carbon granules and can extend the life of the microphone.

If the carbon mic is not the noise-canceling type, ambient noise can enter the voice grill along with your voice sound waves and drown out or overwhelm your transmissions, making them unreadable.

The primary advantages of the carbon mic are low cost, durability, and resistance to radio frequency interference (RFI) and electromagnetic interference (EMI). You can throw this mic around the cockpit without damaging it; in fact that might even help prolong its useful life. This is a good microphone to carry as an inexpensive emergency backup.

Dynamic microphone

The dynamic mic is composed of a wire-wound coil connected to a diaphragm. As the speaker's voice strikes the diaphragm, the coil moves in and out along a core magnet, producing a voltage that is amplified then transmitted. Dynamic mics are heavier than electrets, but they are reliable, virtually immune to RFI, and have excellent frequency response.

Telex 100-T dynamic microphone.

Electret microphone

For noise-canceling microphones, the electret is the best choice. It is small, light, and produces the best voice transmissions. Electret mics are also highly resistant to outside RFI and EMI, inexpensive, and highly reliable.

Electret mics feature a fixed backplate and a charged, mobile plate that moves proportionally to the movement of the diaphragm. The charged/fixed backplate design of the electret mic promotes clear voice transmission. The noise-canceling feature works via an additional port in the mic through which ambient noise can enter. Ambient noise enters through the additional port and hits one side of the diaphragm and simultaneously enters through the voice grille and hits the other side of the diaphragm. Both sources of noise cancel each other out by hitting the front and back sides of the diaphragm equally. This leaves the voice striking only one side of the diaphragm, generating an electrical signal as the distance between the fixed and charged plate varies.

Telex 500T electret microphone.

Microphone problems

Microphone problems are frequently the cause of many transmission complaints, so it's important to learn how to isolate the microphone as the problem before spending too much time and money on other components.

Most avionics shops have a microphone test box for testing keying and modulation. With the mic plugged into the test box, the tech can easily check for intermittent wiring problems by wiggling the cord where it enters the mic and watching the test meter for intermittent operation. If the test needle is slamming over into the red zone on the test meter, the mic is overmodulating and, if possible, needs to be adjusted. The meter will also show if the mic's output is too low for proper transmitter operation.

Here are some other microphone problems you can look for:

Gain adjustment set too high. This occurs when excessive amounts of cockpit noise are being transmitted. Readjust the gain on the microphone and confirm proper reception with someone listening to your transmission. You might run into this problem when installing a new microphone that is different than the old one. If your airplane already has a dynamic, electronically amplified mic, replace it with the same kind of mic. In any case, make sure you check the output quality of a new mic whenever you replace an old one.

Distorted signals. This occurs when the signal develops instability before being transmitted. Causes include speaking too loudly, misadjusted gain, poor quality mic, damaged mic element, or even poorly installed antennas, defective shielding, and poor bonds. The instability introduces other frequencies in the voice signal and changes the character and clarity of the signal.

Your microphone technique may be causing the problem. Placing the mic near the corner of your mouth rather than directly in front of it and close to your lips and speaking at a normal level will reduce the chance of poor transmission. Try an experiment. Using a remote microphone and a tape recorder, speak a 15- to 20-word sentence into the microphone, holding the mic directly in front of your mouth. Try the same sentence again, but this time hold the mic at the corner of your mouth. Now play back the tape and compare the sound on the two sentences. The first sentence, where you held the mic in front of your mouth, will demonstrate the injection of sharp "S," "P," and "T" sounds. The second sentence should be relatively free of such sounds and be distortion free, an important requirement for aircraft transmissions.

Telex aviation microphones.

Defective push-to-talk switch. It's easy to tell if a push-to-talk switch simply isn't working. You won't hear the familiar "click" as you depress the microphone button or the push-to-talk switch. It is much harder to detect a short-circuited push-to-talk switch because such a failure can render your radio inoperative on any frequency. This is also known as a "stuck mic." It can also prevent other aircraft and transmitters within range to be shut off from communicating, so it's important to learn how to detect this problem.

If your airplane has two mic jacks (the receptacles into which you plug the microphone) and they are wired in parallel to each other—quite common in most installations—a shorted mic button on the copilot's side can activate the key line and continuously transmit a carrier signal. This will infuriate everyone trying to use whatever frequency you're transmitting on and prevent you from using your radio.

If you suspect this problem, the easiest way to troubleshoot is to switch microphones. With a good mic on each side, you should be able to transmit and receive normally. This is another good reason to carry a spare microphone. If either the pilot's or copilot's push-to-talk switch is stuck, then you have a real problem and might have to shut your com radios off to prevent blocking everyone's transmissions. This is also a good reason to carry a portable transceiver.

Jack problems. A common microphone installation problem is installers using the incorrect mic jacks. The jack must have the correct detent distance to match the mic plug, otherwise the plug won't make the proper contact and may fall out. To check for this, simply grasp the body of the mic plug and tug gently. If the plug pops out easily, the detent on the tip of the jack is probably not mating with the spring-loaded contact finger on the jack. Even if installers use the correct jacks, the contact finger can become bent or misaligned during subsequent maintenance or normal use.

Although it's better to replace an incorrect, misaligned jack, you can correct a mismatch between the jack's contact finger and the plug by reforming the contact finger on the jack. Remove the plug from the jack and make sure the jack's diameter is compatible with the mic plug. Bend the contact finger down slightly, then back up, then finally back to the horizontal position, which should bring the finger back into alignment with the detent in the tip of the microphone plug. If the misalignment isn't excessive, putting a slight curve in the long contact finger that mates with the plug detent will often do the job.

Intercom jacks should always be installed with a floating ground, which means that the jack itself is insulated from the airframe and not installed so the metal jack can contact the metal on which it's mounted. Use insulating washers to isolate the jack, unless the mounting structure is nonconductive. Then terminate the jack's ground at the intercom. This is the accepted way to reduce potential sources of audio noise.

Wiring problems. The figure shows a dynamic mic opened up for inspection and testing. This is just an example to show you how to test and clean a typical microphone.

Recall that wiring problems can be detected by wiggling the wire where it enters the mic with the mic plugged into a test box. A good indication that the wiring is defective is there is cracked insulation around the microphone cord, especially where it enters the mic.

Mic plug entry

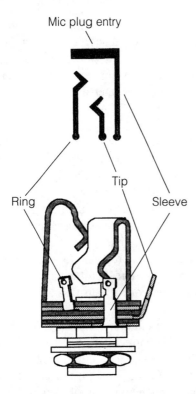

Tip

Ring

Sleeve

Side view of a microphone jack. Terminal and spring-loaded contact for tip and ring are directly across from each other.

After carefully removing the screws from the rear cover, gently lift the mic body away from the front section, exposing the push-to-talk switch and the dynamic element. You'll see where the wires enter the body of the microphone and the push-to-talk (PTT) switch contacts. PTT switch contacts can become contaminated with nicotine if smokers fly in your airplane, plus corrosion can build up on the contacts through normal use. Clean the contacts with some electrical contact cleaner, available at a local electronics store or at a well-stocked pilot shop.

With a volt-ohmmeter, you can test for continuity between various areas to confirm that the wiring is in good shape. There are five places to check on this microphone:

- With one probe on the barrel of the mic jack (the portion nearest the wire) and one probe on the tip, depress the PTT switch. The meter (VOM) should indicate continuity, confirming that the PTT switch is operating correctly and that the key line should work.

- Place one probe on the center section of the jack (ring) and the other where the wire enters the element (from the switch). Again, depress the PTT switch and check for continuity; this confirms one of the audio wires. These first two tests are the only ones where you'll check for continuity while depressing the PTT switch. On the remaining tests, you'll just be checking for continuity between the wires themselves.

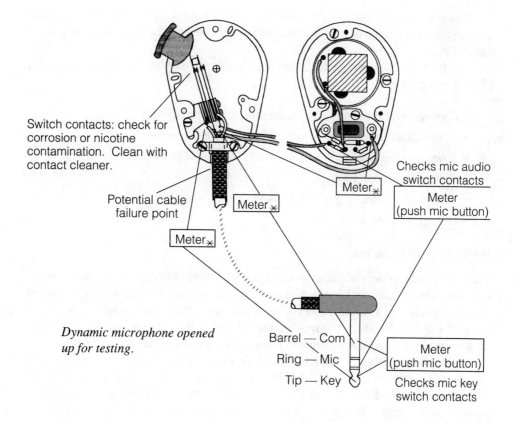

Switch contacts: check for corrosion or nicotine contamination. Clean with contact cleaner.

Potential cable failure point

Checks mic audio switch contacts

Meter (push mic button)

Dynamic microphone opened up for testing.

Barrel — Com
Ring — Mic
Tip — Key

Meter (push mic button)

Checks mic key switch contacts

- You can't test for continuity through the dynamic element, so check from where the wire enters the dynamic element to the ring on the jack to confirm the other audio wire.
- Check continuity from the tip of the jack to the solder joint at the switch.
- Check continuity from the barrel to the solder joint where the cable is clamped to the mic body.

The shielding on the cable terminates at the jack and should be isolated from the jack. If you suspect shielding problems, you can check for continuity between the shield to any part of the jack. There should be no continuity on this test.

If you find a defective wire and feel confident about repairing it, remove the cable and cut it back beyond the damaged area. Remove the outer plastic sheath and determine the length of each wire needed, then cut the wire and strip the insulation from the wire. Pretin the wires and solder to their respective points. Be careful not to use excessive heat, which can easily damage electronic circuitry and plastic parts. Recheck the soldered joints with the VOM and reassemble the microphone. Plug it in and test it by asking the tower or unicom for a radio check.

Some newer microphones like Electro-Voice's have a removable cord. A small plug-in connector at the base of the mic body makes changing a defective cord a much simpler job.

Anytime you have one of the following problems, try a new mic first before going to the avionics shop:

- Com receiver doesn't work. Transmitter might be keyed.
- Com will not transmit. Mic key button might be defective.
- Tower can hear carrier signal, but no voice. Could be broken wire in mic.
- Transmissions intermittent.
- Transmissions weak, garbled, breaking up, or noisy.
- Hum in speaker when mic keyed.

Buying a microphone

There are a wide variety of microphones to choose from. Some are designed for right- or left-handed people, for people with low- or high-pitched voices, and for helicopter versus airplane use. I recommend the most expensive mic you can afford that is designed for aviation and for the type of aircraft you'll be flying most. You'll find the more expensive microphones deliver cleaner audio and long-lasting reliability.

Look for microphones that are TSOed; this assures you the mic meets minimum quality and durability standards. You'll want to make sure your mic has excellent noise-canceling capability, is amplified, adjustable, comfortable to use, and resistant to external interference. Warranty support is also important. Some manufacturers—David Clark is notable for this—support their products for nearly the life of the product, while others aren't so helpful. Ask other pilots and aircraft owners and avionics shops before making the purchase decision.

HEADSETS

Headsets have come a long way from the hard plastic earpieces that used to fit into the classic leather helmet. They are available in a wide range of prices and capabilities, from simple earplug-type lightweight designs to the expensive active noise reduction (ANR) headsets pioneered by Bose and now offered by a number of manufacturers at even more reasonable prices.

There are two basic types of headsets to consider. One is the lightweight that consists of portable headphone-type earpieces that have good sound quality but don't reduce noise at all. The other is the full-blown noise-canceling headset with the large earmuff-type headphones; these offer considerable noise-reduction capability. If you fly airplanes with extremely quiet cockpits, you might find the lightweight headset more comfortable for long trips.

Telex ProAir 2000E headset with electret microphone.

The noise-canceling earmuff headsets do a great job of reducing harmful noise, but they do so by clamping your head in what feels like a vise after a long flight. Be sure to try on a pair before you buy to see if they are comfortable for more than a few minutes. You'll find that headsets with liquid-filled cushions are more comfortable and seal better to your head than headsets with foam-filled cushions. Also, the liquid-filled cushions also mold better to your head if you are wearing glasses. Headsets usually have a noise-reduction rating that is useful for comparing their effectiveness, but nothing beats a trial flight in a noisy airplane.

Active noise reduction (ANR) headsets are becoming more popular, especially now that more manufacturers are entering the business. These work by generating an "antinoise" exactly opposite in phase to the noise coming from the engine, wind noise, etc. The actual noise and the antinoise, if properly generated, cancel each other out, leaving a remarkably quiet environment for your ears. ATC and intercom communications come through loud and clear with ANR headsets, and they are definitely worth the investment if you fly a lot in noisy environments.

ANR headsets can be used as portable headsets if you fly a variety of airplanes. If you own an airplane and are buying ANR headsets, have your avionics shop hard-wire the power source and control module into your panel so you won't have wire spaghetti all over the cockpit. The portable systems use a cigarette lighter plug for power. One benefit of these systems is that if the noise-canceling function stops working, the headset will operate like a normal headset, still protecting your ears from damage, although not quite as comfortably as when the unit was working as designed.

Aircraft headsets are designed for the proper 600-ohm impedance rating for aircraft electronics. Regular stereo headphones aren't designed for the same impedance, and using them could cause damage to the avionics. Sporty's Pilot Shop sells a plug-in impedance-matching device that adapts eight-ohm stereo headphones to the 600-ohm avionics (see Sources at end of book for address and phone number).

David Clark headset with electret microphone.

While most aircraft headsets can be used in any aircraft, some are designed specifically for the high-noise environment in helicopters. Don't waste the extra money for a helicopter headset unless you are flying helicopters.

Aircraft headsets feature most microphone types, but the electret has proven to be the lightest and most reliable for headset use, especially in terms of noise-canceling capability. Headsets with dynamic mics are cheaper but might not give as satisfactory a result. Again, if you can, try before you buy and ask around for advice from fellow pilots.

The same problems that plague microphones cause trouble with headsets. Be careful not to wind your headset wires up too tightly when you're done flying; just let the wires flop loosely in your headset bag to keep them in good shape. Don't leave the headset on an instrument panel on a sunny day. In fact, keep your headset away from the instrument panel altogether because the magnets in the speakers can harm your aircraft's compass.

Many headsets offer easily exchangeable parts, so if you're planning to keep your headset, you may want to buy one that is easily repairable.

INTERCOMS

Nothing will improve the comfort of your airplane when flying with passengers more than a good intercom. Without an intercom, noise from the engine and prop and slipstream will overtax your ears and drown out your voice, causing you and your passen-

Telex 5 x 5 Pro lightweight headset with reversible electret microphone.

gers to yell at each other to be heard. Flight instruction without an intercom is extremely difficult, and it is surprising that most manufacturers do not automatically install intercoms in their training aircraft. Intercoms can make the training experience much more enjoyable and productive, not to mention prevent hearing loss among future pilots.

Cockpit noise levels are usually from 80 to 100 dB, and the average person in airplane environment speaks at 95 dB. If there isn't at least a 10 percent difference between the voice decibel level and the ambient noise level, the voice will be smothered by the noise. So you can see that in some of the noisier aircraft, you must really raise your voice to be heard. It is more than likely that a lot of people have quit flying lessons because the noise and the yelling made the experience so uncomfortable.

Telex PC 4 intercom. This intercom can be mounted horizontally or vertically, taking very little panel space.

An intercom is the least expensive and easiest avionics device to install you'll ever run into. There are a variety of brands available, and you can purchase a good-quality unit for under $200.

Some features to look for in an intercom include:

Voice activation. Most modern intercoms have this feature. When you speak into your microphone, only then does the intercom pick up your voice and transmit it to whoever is connected with you. Outside noise isn't transmitted. If you have a chance to test the intercom before buying, make sure the first few syllables are not cut off before voice activation kicks in.

Number of stations. You can buy intercoms with two, four, or six stations, depending on how many seats are in your airplane and how many seats you want to wire for intercabin communications.

Permanent or temporary installation. If you are, say, a flight instructor who teaches in a variety of nonintercom-equipped aircraft, you might want to buy a pair of headsets and a portable intercom. The same goes if you rent airplanes that don't have intercoms. The drawback to a portable intercom, however, is the proliferation of wires in the cockpit. It's not pretty and you have to be careful not to tangle the wires with something important, like the flight or engine controls. A permanently installed intercom stays with the airplane and cuts down on the number of wires snaking around the cockpit. One disadvantage to the permanent installation is the extra cost of installation. Much of this is due to having to remove lots of upholstery to route new wires.

Separate volume and squelch controls for both pilot and copilot. People have their own comfort levels and will enjoy greater comfort if they can set volume and squelch to their own satisfaction.

Horizontal or vertical panel installation option. This allows flexibility in deciding where to squeeze the intercom into your instrument panel. If you can't install it both ways, you might find that the unit you've chosen won't fit in the only space you have left.

Separate pilot/copilot and passenger circuits. This allows you to shut off the passenger circuit so you and the copilot can communicate without having to listen to the grumbles and groans from your backseat flyers. This can be very useful when you're shooting an approach to minimums.

Intercom installation tips

For a panel-mounted intercom, locate a point on the instrument panel that you can comfortably reach and where there is enough room behind the panel to fit the intercom and some wiring. Usually, you'll find an open spot on the copilot's side of the panel works best. You won't have to actuate the intercom controls that often, so it doesn't need to be right in front of you. If there is absolutely no space at all, you can have your installer build a little bracket to mount the intercom just under the bottom of the panel, as long as it doesn't interfere with your legs and full movement of the controls.

Intercoms usually come with stick-on placards that glue onto the panel after the intercom is installed. Ask your installer if they offer an alternative method of placarding the intercom, like silk screening the panel or making up a laminated plastic tag (see placarding discussion in chapter 4). You want to try to match the intercom installation with the rest of the panel so it looks natural and blends in with your existing avionics.

Ask your installer to use Mil-spec wiring. It is more tolerant to soldering-iron heat and has excellent insulation quality. Some intercom manufacturers supply their own wiring harnesses with their products. Don't use them until you and your tech have inspected the wire and the quality of the solder joints and determine that the quality is better than what the installer can build.

If the intercom manufacturer recommends that mic and phone jacks be lifted above ground (not grounded directly to the mounting surface or instrument panel), consult your installer to make sure that's how the jacks are installed. This requirement prevents noise from entering the audio system via the grounded panel, especially in the case where the bonding of the panel to the airframe becomes loose, deteriorates, or is accidentally removed during maintenance.

Intercom wiring should not be tied or mounted to any heavy current-carrying cables like the large cables going to the battery or to pulse equipment coaxial cables (transponder and DME coax). Routing intercom wires close to these cables could be a major source of noise.

It might be possible to route the intercom bundle next to the main electrical harness running from the instrument panel back to some remote-mounted electronics in the back of the airplane. But this could also result in some interference, so if intercom wires are routed next to the main harness, they should be attached in such a way that they are easy to move later if noise becomes a problem.

To ensure backup operation in case of intercom failure, the audio amplifier should be wired directly to a set of mic and headphone jacks labeled "Emergency Mic/ Phone." This will allow normal operation of the radios using the spare hand mic you'll always be carrying. All audio wires should be twisted, shielded pairs for optimum noise suppression, with the shielding terminating at the source radio.

Intercom jack installation

When consulting with your installer about where to place your rear-seat headphone and mic jacks, don't just opt for the most convenient spot. Many installers, for example, like to remove the ashtrays from the sidewall in modern Piper singles and twins and install a little plate in place of the ashtrays.

More important, however, is whether the installer's recommended jack placement will work. Take the ashtray example. Have you ever sat in the back seat of a Piper wearing a headset plugged into jacks where the ashtrays used to be? I've found this is a big mistake many owners make. The back-seat passengers might find their shoulders pushing up against the jacks, making them uncomfortable, especially if there are two people in the back seat, and this can damage the headphone plugs and ashtray jacks.

A better solution for Pipers is to install a doubler in the overhead air-vent tunnel that runs along the ceiling. Install the jacks in that tunnel. This way, the jacks are easy to reach and don't get in anyone's way. If that is too many headphone wires dangling in the air for your comfort, another option is to install the jacks on the aft baggage compartment bulkhead. That way the wires can rest along the back of the seat, with excess wire stuffed into the baggage compartment.

Remember that it's up to you, the owner, to make these decisions. You're the one that is going to have to live with the installation for a long time. Some installers initially opt for the easy solution, like replacing the ashtrays, so it's up to you to make your ergonomic tests and make your desires known.

Perform a final test of the intercom installation by powering up your avionics. Turn on the ADF and tune in a station's audio or a radio station plus ATIS on one of the com radios. When you key the microphone, the audio from both sources should mute. Intercom audio levels do need to be calibrated to the aircraft and microphone you're using, so make sure the installer does this as a normal part of the installation.

SPEAKERS

Speaker operation is relatively simple. A small wire coil inside a magnet vibrates whenever a voltage from an amplifier is applied. The coil is attached to a paper cone, and when the coil vibrates, it makes the cone vibrate. The vibrating cone creates sound waves that the pilot hears as a voice from the speaker.

Speaker problems

It frequently occurs that a pilot doesn't even notice their speaker has stopped working because they were using headsets and never used the speaker. It's a good idea to check the speaker occasionally to make sure it's working because it is a backup for your headset, just as the headphones are a backup for the speaker.

If the speaker is suspect, plug in your headset and listen for clear and undistorted audio. If the audio is low from either radio, you'll have to have the radio checked, but if it is low when listening to the speaker, and not when using the headset, then the speaker is the problem.

Speaker installation tips

Speakers should be high quality, high frequency, and mounted in rigid frames to prevent warping and distortion. The speaker should be able to handle continuous power application with no more than 10 percent distortion. If replacing a speaker, make sure it has the correct impedance for the application.

Speaker wiring should be routed away from alternating current circuits such as certain types of lighting circuits and windshield heat inverters. Speakers should not be grounded to the airframe right next to the speaker but should be grounded as close to the audio source as possible, to prevent unwanted noise from sneaking in via the airframe. Make sure that any insulation surrounding the speaker isn't conductive and that the insulation hasn't been stuffed too close to the speaker inhibiting the movement of the cone.

Finally, having two speakers, one for the pilot and one for the copilot, promotes accurate communications.

MICROPHONE, HEADSET, ANR HEADSET, AND INTERCOM MANUFACTURERS

These manufacturers' addresses are listed in the Sources section at the end of this book. Also see headset manufacturers.

Microphones

Electro-Voice

Flightcom

Telex Communications

Headsets

Acousticom

Aire-Sciences

Audio Com

Aviation Communications

Aviall

Comtronics

Concept Industries

David Clark

Evolution

Flightcom

McCoy Avionics

MicroCom

Oregon Aero

Peltor

Pilot Avionics

Plantronics

Puritan-Bennett Aero Systems (oxygen mask with mic)

Radio Systems Technology (comes in kit form or factory-built)

Senheiser Electronics

Sigtronics
Softcom
Sony
Telex Communications

ANR Headsets

Bose
David Clark
Evolution
Telex

Intercoms

Audio Com
Aviation Communications
Bendix/King
David Clark
Comtronics
Concept Industries
Flightcom
McCoy Avionics
MicroCom
Pilot Avionics
PS Engineering
Radio Systems Technology
Sigtronics
Telex Communications

6
Audio and noise

YOU MIGHT FIND THAT YOUR PERCEPTION OF HOW WELL YOUR RADIOS
work is affected by the amount of unwanted noise and interference you have to
listen to while using your radios. This chapter explains some of the sources of unwanted noise and some of the ways good avionics technicians prevent noise and interference using good installation techniques.

AUDIO SYSTEM

The audio system can be as simple as an internal amplifier in the navcom unit wired to
a common point and switchable from, say, com 1 to com 2 with mini switches. Or in
the case of a one-radio airplane, the amplifier can be wired directly to the speaker and
headphones.

More common, especially in IFR-equipped aircraft, is the panel-mounted amplifier with built-in switching (commonly called an audio panel) or a panel-mounted set
of switches connected to a remotely installed amplifier. The job of these amplifiers is
to receive low audio (which is basically a weak signal transmitted over many miles),
isolate it, send it to the switch-selected output (headphones or speaker), and amplify it
so that you can hear what somebody is trying to tell you.

Audio panels tie together multiple inputs to let you use them all efficiently. Instead of having to turn the ADF volume up every time you want to listen to a station, you simply flip the ADF's audio panel switch to either speaker or headphone and listen. This saves wear and tear on volume controls and gives you a central black box from which you can control all your radios' audio.

The easiest unit to install and maintain is the panel-mounted audio panel. Examples of these are King's KMA134 and KMA24, Narco's CP-136, and the former Collins AMR-350 (note: Collins sold its line of Micro Line avionics to S-TEC). Radio Systems Technology makes an audio panel kit you can build.

Panel-mounted King KMA24H audio panel.

AUDIO SYSTEM PROBLEMS

Any kind of switch is always a potential source of trouble, and audio panels have lots of switches. When squawking audio problems, be sure you have the switches set correctly before taking the time and trouble to have someone work on your system. It's all too common for flight instructors to fail to teach students the details of how audio panels are set up. If you rent airplanes, especially ones with different avionics setups, take a few minutes to learn the various audio panels so you eliminate lack of knowledge as a source of problems.

In my experience, audio panels with toggle switches are more reliable than those with push-button switches. Other sources of trouble in audio systems are the switching circuits used to gain the most efficient use of the audio. Without this switching, you'd have to turn down the volume on other pieces of avionics any time you wanted to transmit to prevent the other audio from interfering with your transmission. The other radios are still producing audio, but it is prevented from reaching the speaker or headphones by muting circuitry. If the wiring or relays that form the heart of the switching and muting circuits are less than perfect, failures might result.

Following are some common audio problems. Reasons for the failure might involve more than just the audio system, and you might see these same problems discussed in another chapter.

Noisy reception. Check for an antenna problem. Or it could simply be a weak or noisy received signal.

Distorted or garbled reception. Check speaker first, then radio, audio amplifier, and associated wiring. If the audio panel uses push-button switches, they could be the problem. Toggle-switch failures are rare. Check for contamination, loose pins, or broken wires on the audio panel mating connector.

Intermittent reception. This problem can be caused by problems with the radio's power wire, grounds, defective pins on the radio's mating connector, problems with the radio itself, or damaged wiring from recent upholstery work. Check to see if the com radio has an intermittent or defective mic being keyed. This would kill all audio if the mic key button is depressed or has failed. Many technicians test for intermittent audio by turning on the ADF audio and listening to it while proceeding with other tests. If the intermittent audio reception problem occurs, the tech will immediately hear the failure when the ADF audio quits. From there, the tech should be able to isolate the problem further, but at least they will have heard the problem and won't ask you to come back later when it gets worse.

Total audio failure. Check for the same items as with intermittent reception. But also check to see if you're trying to listen on the speaker with the audio panel set to headphones. Also, make sure the "auto" switch hasn't been moved from where you normally set it. This happens more often than most pilots would like to admit.

Weak reception. If noise isn't a problem but reception is still weak, check the radio or audio amplifier.

Weak transmission. This could be from a bad mic, radio, or antenna.

Mic key line working (able to transmit carrier) but no modulation (but cannot transmit voice). Mic jack contacts might be defective or mic wiring defective. Try replacing with a new mic.

Whine. A whining sound could be interference from alternator or electric motors (like a motor-driven rotating beacon).

Motorboating. This is noise in the system that sounds like a motorboat engine. It could be caused by open ground wires, bad grounds, or a miscalibrated radio.

Static. Static can result if the shielding between audio wires is touching. Or P-static is from friction building up due to action of air and precipitation molecules on the airframe. Check that all static wicks are in good shape (they do wear out) and that control surfaces and other hinged surfaces like gear doors are properly bonded to the airframe.

NOISE

We would all like our audio systems to be totally noise free, but we'll always have to put up with a certain amount of interference. Even the best designed and installed systems will pick up some noise from the atmosphere and from other electrical components in the airplane. You need to know what is normal and what isn't for your particular installation so you don't waste time troubleshooting something that doesn't need fixing.

The alternator (center, belt-driven unit) can be a source of noise problems for a variety of avionics equipment.

One simple way of avoiding noise problems is to install avionics of the same brand. Mismatched black boxes can introduce unwanted noise that is difficult to eliminate, although even a full panel of, say, King avionics can still cause problems from poor wiring or installation.

Most sources of noise are readily identified but still difficult to track down because of the many routes the noise can take to arrive at the radio and disrupt communications or navigation. Some causes of noise are obvious enough to isolate and reduce to acceptable levels, but others are harder to find and even harder to fix.

How does one deal with those annoying and possibly dangerous phenomena? Even new "glass cockpits" with multiple cathode-ray tube displays in the panel suffer from distortion and interference like irritating hums, whines, and popping noises in the audio.

Knowledge is the answer to improving our ability to search out and destroy radio interference. The aircraft environment is a hotbed of interference from motors, generators, alternators, strobe lights, and poorly installed radios. To make it more complicated, nature has seen fit to blanket the airplane with atmospheric and precipitation static, lightning, and even sunspot activity.

Each of the following potential noise generators can radiate RFI or induce electrical signals directly or indirectly into an avionics radio. The sources of noise are divided into three general groups:

- atmospheric static
- precipitation or P-static
- man-made avionics noise (the worst of the bunch)

Don't expect solutions to all of the problem areas mentioned; however, you will come away with enough ideas that will help you and your technician map out an approach to minimize or eliminate unwanted noise signals.

Atmospheric static

Atmospheric static is caused by RF energy produced by electrical discharges in the atmosphere. Its effects can be effectively controlled through proper use of directional antennas, RF bonding, and internal radio filtering.

P-static

P-static results when an aircraft passes through clouds, rain, dust, and other particles suspended in the atmosphere. You might be surprised to know how much dirt there is floating around in the air we breathe. P-static is also known as *friction charging* and occurs when electrons are stripped off the airframe's skin, changing the electrical potential of the airframe. When the static charge discharges suddenly, you can hear P-static as a hiss or frying sound in the audio, or see it displayed as nervous navigation needles, or even experience blanking of communications.

Proper use of static wicks and good bonding procedures on antennas and airframe grounds can keep P-static effects within acceptable limits. You can obtain additional protection by ensuring correct routing, shielding, and bonding of wiring harnesses and antennas.

Another important bonding factor is control surfaces and other hinged surfaces attached to the airframe. While most control surfaces have a metal-to-metal connection to the airframe, static built up on, say, the right wing might not flow into the right aileron to discharge from the static wicks on the trailing edge of that aileron because of lubricant and dirt buildup on the hinges. You've probably seen the bonding straps that electrically "attach" the aileron to the wing, and you probably were shown to check those during preflight inspections. These bonding straps do wear out and fall off, so it is important to keep them in good shape. Problems with the bonding straps can crop up after paint jobs. If the control surfaces were removed for painting and rebalancing (which conscientious paint shops will do as a normal part of the job), someone might either leave the bonding strap off completely or reattach it on top of the fresh paint, instead of removing the paint where the strap attaches to ensure a good metal-to-metal bond.

For long-term protection, do not ignore the condition of your airplane's static wicks. These devices are designed to discharge the electrical potential built up by flying through P-static-generating atmosphere, and their effectiveness diminishes over time. Next time you go flying, look at the static wicks. The discharging occurs at the tail end of the wick, and if the tail is missing a lot of its brushy ends or is broken off completely, it can't do its job. Unfortunately, many mechanics ignore static wicks during routine inspections and never call for their replacement. Keeping static wicks in good shape is especially important on some of the fast, modern, single-engine aircraft like Piper's Malibu and the turbine-powered TBM 700.

A good example of a bonding problem occurred to one of my customers in southern California. Many pilots and technicians aren't aware that a major cause of P-static is dust, not just moisture like snow and rain. Range on this customer's nav receivers was merely 30 to 40 miles, well below what it should be. Rather than try one thing and test fly it and then try another repair and another test flight, we decided to shotgun the airframe's bonding by rebonding all antennas, control surfaces, and hinged surfaces like gear doors. The results were outstanding: nav range more than doubled to over 100 miles. At the time, there was a severe drought in California, which resulted in a lot of dust suspended in the atmosphere, even at higher altitudes. (We didn't just jump at the bonding problem initially; the first step in a nav problem is always to recalibrate the units as close as possible to factory specifications before trying another more expensive fix.)

Thunderstorms can create conditions that generate emissions from the extremities of an aircraft, commonly referred to as "Saint Elmo's fire." These emissions are displayed as corona and streamer discharges and usually last for only a few minutes. Streamers can grow from 20 to 30 feet long but usually don't contribute to significant navigational difficulties unless antennas aren't well bonded to the airframe. Saint Elmo's fire was named for Saint Peter Gonzalez (don't ask me how you get Elmo from Peter Gonzalez) who lived in the 13th century and was named the patron saint of Mediterranean sailors. The discharge is said to be a sign of Saint Elmo's protection, so I suppose pilots can take it as such, too, being sailors of the atmosphere.

Another factor that can contribute to airframe charging is exhaust from the engines. Positive or negative ions (atoms having a positive or negative charge) are selectively drawn to the exterior cowling by the exhaust, creating either a negative or positive charge that migrates to the airframe. The amount of this charging is directly related to throttle settings and the diameter and length of the exhaust stack.

Once part of the airframe develops an electrical potential, either from friction, thunderstorms, or engine charging, interference or noise can be generated three ways:

- corona
- streamer discharge
- sparkover from surfaces that aren't bonded to each other

Corona discharges cover the RF spectrum from very low frequency (VLF) to high frequency (HF) and can significantly affect very-high frequency (VHF) and ultra-high frequency (UHF) communications used by avionics. Aircraft antennas are ideal extremities, protuberance, or sharp points that have the potential to discharge the charge collected on the airframe surface.

Here you have an avionics system, from antenna to radio, subjected to considerably more current than it was ever designed to handle. Large portions of the charge are discharged harmlessly into the atmosphere, but a small, sometimes lethal dosage can reach the radio. If not damaged, the radio most likely will shut down due to the RF and IF stages being driven into oscillation and saturation. If you suspect this has happened, look for small, needle-like black dots on the surface of the antenna. These are penetration points—a telltale sign that possible damage has occurred. Note that this damage can also be caused by small tendrils of charges from lightning strikes. Discharges from control surfaces, nose cones, wing tips, and other unbonded surfaces can corrupt radio reception or transmission on aircraft smaller than light jets because the antennas are in close proximity to the unbonded surfaces.

Plastic windshields, wing tips, vertical fin caps, and other plastic fairings are sources of *streamer discharge*. During flight, the windshield, for example, builds a charge due to frictional interface with dust, moisture, or precipitation, and the charge continues to build until it jumps across to the metal airframe. Once the streamer begins, it will continue as long as the charge is maintained. Few people are aware that some waxes are prone to streamer production, so you might want to check this with the wax manufacturer or stop using a particular wax if you suspect that it's causing a streamer problem.

Tips on preventing P-static

Follow these guidelines to prevent P-static buildup.

- Use proper antenna spacing as recommended by manufacturers.
- Ensure the antenna base is properly bonded to the airframe skin. That means you need metal-to-metal contact, with no paint or other insulating substances between the base of the antenna and the skin of the aircraft.
- Antennas usually shouldn't be installed within three feet of the windshield, although it is frequently easier for installers to do so. It is more difficult to install an antenna a proper distance from the windshield because access to the airframe skin is harder, plus antenna cables have a longer run to the radios, but the extra effort will be worthwhile. The expense of relocating a badly placed antenna will exceed the initial cost to do it right the first time.
- As a general rule, you can minimize the P-static noise problems by making sure there is metal-to-metal contact between all access doors, antennas, and onboard equipment, whether avionics or electrical. If not installed, bonding straps should be added to control surfaces. If this is very difficult, the chances of noise prob-

lems ocurring will be much lower if there is less than ¼ Ω resistance between the control surface or gear door and the airframe.

Don't ignore inspection panels as a potential source of noise, too. Panels need to be bonded to the airframe as well. Usually, the panels are metal and are bonded through normal installation. Metal screws attach the panel to the metal airframe. If there isn't bare metal-to-metal contact, however, the panel isn't bonded and could be a source of noise.

- Radio racks should be bonded with at least two, 1-inch-by-5-inch-long straps connected between the radio rack and airframe ground. If possible, also have the mounting base of the rack RF bonded; this will doubly improve the bonding and ensure the installation to be free from the troubling effects of extraneous RF interference.

This doesn't seem to be complicated, does it? Just throw on a few bonding straps, check this and that, and that solves your problems. The truth is, these considerations are frequently ignored in the field. Most of the aircraft I've evaluated over the last two years were in dire need of the techniques explained above. Avionics and maintenance shop managers need to advise their customers about the necessity for good RF bonding. It is something that should be done during a normal installation, checked as part of a routine inspection, and should not be ignored.

Man-made noise

Being familiar with noise sources is a giant step toward preventing unwanted signals from entering the audio or causing navigation signal problems. The problems that arise are frequently the result of lack of adequate information. Attempting to troubleshoot a problem without being prepared might result in a technician setting off in the wrong direction and wasting time and money and not fixing the original problem.

There are many sources of man-made noise. The following explains many of these sources and what can be done to minimize or eliminate them.

Wiring is one of the weak components of avionics systems and can be divided into four categories:

- AC (alternating current) power
- DC (direct current) power
- pulse circuits (transponder and DME)
- sensitive circuits (autopilot feedback circuits)

Interference or noise signals can be divided into three categories:

- electrical fields
- magnetic fields
- RF (radio frequency) fields

Strobe lights can be a major source of avionics noise. The noise generated is nonselective and can penetrate virtually any radio.

These signals, in turn, can be injected into three potentially sensitive areas of an avionics system either via

- antennas
- power lines (wires)
- signal lines

There are four coupling modes you should know about:

- conductive
- capacitive
- inductive
- electromagnetic (RF)

Coupling, the introduction of unwanted signals or noise into electric and electronic circuits, occurs in about 88 percent of all aircraft wiring. For the most part, coupling effects are neutralized by circuit design, wire separation, and other rigorous installation practices. Power lines, AC/DC relays, and solenoid lines are key concerns for coupling interference into analog, digital, and audio signal lines. Conductive, inductive, and capacitive coupling take place via magnetic fields cutting across equipment and wiring. Electromagnetic coupling is RF entering through antennas.

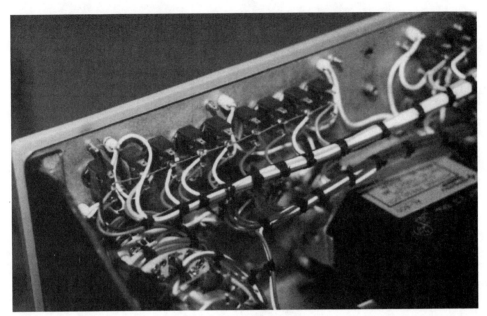

Here is a potential noise-entry point to the avionics system. All radio wiring in the panel is unshielded.

A good example of a simple noise problem is the complaint of noise in the speaker from one of the radios. This could be due to low voltage. Most radios are designed to operate within specified input voltages. A 12-volt aircraft, for example, might have radios that specify input voltage from 11 to 14 volts. Low voltage could prevent the radio's circuitry from operating efficiently and could allow the generation of noise internally or into the audio system.

To check for this, you can simulate a low-voltage condition by testing your radio's reception on the ground with the avionics on but without the engine running. As you turn on more and more electric items, the bus voltage will drop below the battery's normal 12 volts (24 volts if it's a 24-volt system). As the voltage drops, you probably will hear noise in the speaker. You can measure the voltage drop by simply checking the bus voltage with a voltmeter attached to the bus bar under the instrument panel, where all the circuit breakers are attached.

If you are getting noise from your speaker, then make sure your alternator or generator is properly charging your electrical system. If the system is charging properly (usually two volts above system voltage for a 12-volt system and four volts above for a 24-volt system), then you won't waste time chasing a noise problem that is caused by low voltage. Keep in mind that if you are troubleshooting a noise problem using battery power alone, you can easily drop the battery below its nominal voltage during testing. Always use a strong, fully charged battery for testing, or better yet, use an external power source to eliminate low voltage as a cause of a radio problem.

There are times when the radio's power supply will suffer a component failure and work fine with operating voltage (14 or 28 volts) applied but act up when the alternator is off-line or when running the radio without the engine and alternator running using battery voltage (12 or 24 volts or less, depending on the battery's charge). It might be embarrassing to find that you wasted several hours troubleshooting a problem that simply was a result of a defective power supply or low voltage. Power converters that convert 12 volts to 24 volts have been known to cause this type of problem.

Relays and solenoids have been sources of radio noise in the past, but this hasn't been a problem with modern aircraft. If an undesirable noise occurs only when you flick a switch or activate a certain circuit, then you can trace the noise to a worn relay or switch contacts. The spark created by the opening and closing of the switch contacts is most likely entering the audio through the wiring attached to the switch.

Inductors, such as solenoids and relay coils, tend to create high voltage transients when their magnetic fields collapse as the circuit feeding the coil is opened. The magnetic lines of flux in the collapsing field will induce a high voltage back into the DC relay coil, which then races back into the system wiring, possibly causing damage to solid-state equipment or noise in the audio. To prevent this, a diode is installed across the coil of the relay. This prevents the voltage produced by the collapsing field to radiate to surrounding wiring, and tends to increase the life of the coil.

Strobe lights are frequent sources of noise complaints, causing loud popping sounds in the marker beacon, navigation, and ADF audio. Because strobes are RF generators by design, it's no wonder thousands of aircraft are plagued by strobe noise squawks. The noise can be transmitted directly to nearby antennas or induced into electrical or radio cables routed too closely to strobe power supplies or strobe power wires. Shielding cables and wires or filtering strobe power supplies can eliminate most of these problems, and so can simply relocating the antenna, the strobe power supply, or in some cases replacing the strobe light with an attenuated version to reduce the radiated interference that emanates from the light.

If the power supply is causing the noise problem, replacing the power supply or installing additional filters might be the only solution. Most strobe manufacturers will overhaul strobe power supplies for a reasonable price, so the simplest solution might be to box up the power supply and send it to the manufacturers. Ask the company to let you know if the condition of the power supply could have caused your noise problem.

Filters

There are four kinds of filters:

- low-pass
- high-pass
- bandpass
- band elimination

Most filters used in noise suppression are the low-pass variety. Filters suppress noise by shunting the undesired energy or noise through a capacitor to ground. To protect the capacitor's dielectric material, the capacitor must have a voltage of at least twice that of the circuit voltage circuit to which it is connected. If electrolytic-type capacitors are used, I recommend a voltage rating of four times the circuit voltage due to potential dielectric failure.

Don't go overboard with filter capacitance, though. Capacitance is measured in microfarads (μF), and although a filter with 1 μF capacitance is ten times as effective as a 0.1 μF capacitor in practice, the small capacitor is more effective at higher frequencies. So it's important to match the filter to the frequency of the unwanted signal you're attempting to eliminate.

The most frequently used filters are low-pass filters with cutoff frequencies in the region of 1 to 10 kilohertz. They have a very small insertion loss for DC circuits and ordinary power-frequency currents, and they can aggressively attenuate all radio interference currents.

One relatively simple way to locate the course of the noise and determine the purity of the DC feed and return lines is with an oscilloscope. Every noise has its own unique signature. Keep in mind that the technician might not want to use a filter for the exact value that is a direct computation of the noise trace as indicated on the oscilloscope. The technician needs to attenuate the offending frequency, and that could lie at a point slightly above or below the center of the noise's frequency range observed on the scope. Many factors affect the frequency transmitted by the source of the noise such as length of wires, capacitive effect due to wire routing, and engine RPM if the noise is related to the generator or alternator. Experimentation may be needed to find a filter to eliminate a specific noise.

FINDING AND ELIMINATING NOISE

Few avionics shops have elaborate signal analyzers, so process of elimination is the only inexpensive and practical way to locate positively the source of an offending noise. Begin by positioning the airplane well away from fluorescent lights, power transformers, operating cars, and other aircraft.

Start the engines, turn on the avionics and other electrical items, and listen to the headset or speaker for the offending noise. If you can't hear it, operate the controls in the aircraft as if you were flying to see if control surfaces or cables are causing the noise. Turn on the autopilot and run it through its ground tests to see if it is making the noise. Continue by running the engines up to maximum RPM, then vary the RPM up and down, slowly, while listening for the elusive suspect. Operate the cowl flaps, fuel pumps, and other intermittently used equipment. If you need to test fly the airplane to find the noise, try various combinations of equipment used while flying to bring out the conditions that lead to the noise generation.

Some of the most often ignored sources of noise generation are improper bonding or grounding of equipment chassis or racks, shielding terminations, common ground tie points, and resistance/inductive effects.

Here are some tips to prevent or eliminate noise problems.

Reduce the possibility of interference coupling by making sure the rack holding the radio and the radio itself are at the same or close to the same potential. Grounds from avionics equipment should have the same ground potential as other radios in the aircraft, whenever possible.

Shielded wiring between the radios should have the shielding terminated no further than 1.5 inches from the connector, and only at one end of the wire. The attaching shielding pigtail must be less than 6 inches long.

Make sure all wiring is capable of carrying the current rating of the equipment to which it is attached.

Transient or spike frequencies are usually found in the 10 Hz frequency range, while continuous noise interference is usually greater than the 10 Hz range. Select filters based on this data.

Digital circuits or lines, which are found more frequently now in advanced avionics equipment, are very sensitive to interference and should be made of twisted-pair or twisted-shielded-pair wiring.

When power-line impedances are in the 10-ohm range and the digital and audio impedances are in the 1000-ohm range, then the power circuit conductors can be unshielded and audio line conductors shielded.

Ask your technician to make sure low-voltage lines are not running close to high-voltage lines and communication lines are not too close to DC or AC power lines.

In most cases, a one-to-five ratio should be used on all bonding straps for RF cancellation. These should be made of flat brass or beryllium/brass stock. The combination of certain lengths of non-RF-type bonding straps such as braided cables, or simply wires and the capacitance caused by other metal sections of the installation, can create circumstances that will produce resonant RF radiation in the 50 to 500 MHz range. This range covers the frequencies used for communication and navigation and thus could cause just the type of interference you don't need.

If you have consistent static in the speaker, it could be caused by a failure of the squelch circuit, or the squelch might not have been set to a muting position. You'll always hear noise in a radio from all kinds of man-made and natural sources. The squelch circuit is designed to mute out the static until a strong clear signal—the signal that you want to hear—is received.

Signals such as those between the autopilot computer and servos and flight director should not be wired to travel through the shielding of the interfacing wires. Never allow equipment racks or their chassis and the attaching harness shields to be used for signal returns. For proper delivery of signals between equipment, use shielded, twisted-pair wires with no less than six twists per inch, or use balanced coaxial lines. This will ensure than any unwanted voltages generated (noise) will cancel each other out. The induced voltage from one wire into another will be 180 degrees out of phase and is therefore neutralized.

When using high- and low-signal wires in an avionics system, treat them like oil and water: they don't mix. Make sure they are routed and tied out separately. To reiterate: each signal line should have its own return line, independent of any other, running as close as possible to the signal line, preferably as a shielded twisted pair of wires. The shielded twisted pair fits the bill and is the best choice.

Shielding is effective only against capacitive-coupled noise sources. These types of noise are produced by power sources like alternators or even inverters (which change voltage from DC to AC, like 12 volts DC to 110 volts AC). Before searching for shielding problems, take a close look for poor grounding of the alternator or a bad alternator filter (the capacitor attached to the alternator). The ADF can be shut down completely by a defective alternator diode; this can generate a frequency close to one of the local radio stations. Crossing power wires at 90 degrees will reduce the effects of capacitive coupling. Also, distance between cabling will dramatically reduce coupling, both capacitive and magnetic. The distance doesn't have to be a great amount, even as much as half an inch can virtually eliminate most of the coupling effects.

You can separate power cables yourself easily using nylon ties obtainable from any electronics store. One method is to make a figure eight around the two cables, then secure the intersection of the eight with a second tie. A better method is to cut a small half-inch piece of rubber tubing and place it between the two cables. With a nylon tie, form a single loop around the first cable, then bring the end of the tie through the tube, around the second cable, and back through the tube. Now insert the end of the tie into the locking part of the tie and pull snug. You now have a half-inch standoff securely holding the two cables apart.

Differences in potential between components or between the instrument panel and instruments are significant targets for noise or adverse signal generation. For example, if an electric gyro should start up and there is a voltage potential between the panel and the gyro, a momentary or even continuous voltage will exist. To check this, hook up your voltmeter to read system voltage on the electrical bus. With the engine running and all electrical equipment and radios on, move the selector on your voltmeter to the lowest voltage range until the lowest reading is showing on the meter. This voltage is your interference. Now you can turn off each piece of electrical or avionics equipment and see which one makes the low voltage go away. That equipment is your culprit. If you don't see any voltage on the voltmeter except for system voltage, then leave the setting on system voltage and watch the needle (or number, if it's a digital readout) for sudden surges as you turn off and on each piece of equipment. A surge will indicate a potential noise-generating piece of equipment. If the panel shares its common ground with another audio component or the microphone circuits, a direct coupling could take place, and it will have to be tracked down if you don't want to have to put up with the interference.

If you suspect inadequate bonding at a given radio, check with a VOM designed to measure below 1 Ω. You'll most likely find primer or corrosion between the radio rack or tray and where they attach to the panel's structure. Just cleaning the mating surfaces isn't enough—you must corrosion-proof the surface as well. Use Alodine solution for aluminum, which is the material you're most likely to find in aircraft avionics installations.

Many technicians encounter autopilot interference problems due to poorly bonded equipment racks to airframe grounds. Routing heavy current-carrying cables next to signal wires can induce random spikes that can make for a frenzied situation for the pilot, especially if it happens on a climb using the autopilot. The airplane can lurch either up or down, right or left, suddenly and momentarily, and sometimes for longer durations, possibly causing loss of control. Finding this problem can be easy or quite difficult, depending on the autopilot or the airplane. Isolation of the problem is easier if you can determine that the source of the problem is caused by, say, keying of the mic or operation of some other piece of avionics. Here are some ideas that you and your technician should consider when troubleshooting autopilot interference problems:

- Place a filter on the generating source of interference.
- Reroute heavy-current leads.
- Bond computer rack properly.
- Bond servo properly.
- Shorten ground leads.
- Reroute communications coax cables away from autopilot signal wiring.
- Relocate any offending antennas.
- Bond antennas to airframe properly.
- Relocate autopilot computer from source of interference.
- Bond any surrounding access covers (near autopilot components) that might be building up static charges.

Exposing contributors to the noise dilemma is half of the battle of calming the torrent of noise that pervades modern avionics equipment. Poor troubleshooting without good solid problem-solving tactics can be expensive. Strapping on a fully loaded arsenal of knowledge before simply replacing components will enhance the odds of success.

AUDIO PANEL MANUFACTURERS

Some audio panel manufacturers are listed as follows. See Sources for addresses.

Bendix/King

Narco

Radio Systems Technology

S-TEC

Sigma-Tek

Terra Avionics

7
Antennas

THIS CHAPTER DISCUSSES ANTENNA POLARIZATION, HOW TO CHOOSE AN antenna, and troubleshooting and rebonding antennas.

ANTENNA POLARIZATION

Ever wonder why your nav antennas are horizontally aligned with the ground, and com antennas point vertically? It's because the radio signals are polarized, sort of like polarized sunglasses where only certain types of light are let through the lens. Nav signals are polarized so that the signal that reaches the receiving nav antenna is horizontally polarized, or parallel the earth's surface. The antenna's horizontal mounting makes it able to better pick up the horizontally polarized signals.

The vertically polarized signals that travel to the com antenna are "ignored" by the horizontally positioned nav antenna but picked up by the vertically mounted com antenna.

WHICH ANTENNA

The best antenna for each piece of avionics on your aircraft is probably the antenna recommended by the avionics manufacturer. Don't shortchange yourself on antennas when having new radios installed, because without a good antenna, your expensive radios will be useless. More details on antenna are given in the chapters on each type of equipment.

ANTENNA PROBLEMS

Checking the aircraft's antenna system is fairly easy and should be done on a regular basis to prevent unscheduled failures. Have a shop place an RF wattmeter in-line of the coaxial cable going to the antenna, and rotate the slug to indicate flow toward the antenna. Select a test frequency. Key the mic and begin to speak. The watt meter should indicate power out and modulation.

RF watt meter. The black, finned object on the right is a dummy load. The interface box on the left allows sampling to an oscilloscope. The black coaxial cable is from the output of a com radio.

If power out is displayed on the meter, the next step is determining if the carrier wave can be modulated when you talk. Blow or whistle into the microphone and observe the power out reading for rapid variations. This will give you a good idea that the transmitter should be transmitting the carrier wave and any verbalizations. If there is no sign of power out and the radio was working before testing, a connection error has occurred or a connector has failed.

Radio transmissions are electromagnetic fields, and they have two field components. One is the *H-field* or *magnetic component*. The other is the *E-field* or electrostatic/capacitive element. H-field antennas are designed to receive magnetic radio signals that are less susceptible to P-static interference; however by their very design, they are prone to noise effects from 400-cycle AC. Coil wound on a ferrite core, H-field antennas are very efficient for receiving radio signals and also induced alternating current. Horizontally polarized antennas such as the navigation balanced loop antenna and Omega system antennas are H-field types.

A combined loop/sense antenna has an H-field component, which is the loop portion, and an E-field component, which is the sense antenna. Vertically polarized antennas such as communications, loran, DME, and transponder antennas are E-field types and are designed to receive electrostatic/capacitive radio waves. These antennas are usually configured to form either a plate or rod shape. Take a look at any com antenna on a Beech, Cessna, or Piper single and you'll see either a blade or rod antenna mounted on the top or bottom of the fuselage. These are E-field antennas. Most of the towel-bar navigation antennas are balanced loop H-field antennas; however, the V-shaped rod or gullwing style nav antennas found on vertical stabilizers are E-field antennas and should be replaced whenever possible.

Antenna systems are often consistent causes of avionics failures. Problems caused by antennas can include intermittent transmission and reception, hum, distortion, or breakup. As with most avionics troubleshooting, begin the process with the simple items like the microphone.

RF coupling can be caused by a defective antenna or coaxial cable or poor bonding of the antenna. Each possible source of trouble must be eliminated until you find the problem. Bond the antenna; did the transmission or reception improve?

Inspect the antenna. Look for small but obvious cracks on the surface of the antenna—there could be hundreds. These cracks admit moisture, destroying the ability of the antenna to function within its design parameters. Replacement is the only option as field repairs are not practical nor recommended. Some shops sand the antenna, fill the cracks, and repaint. This isn't a good idea, because paint will most likely reduce the effectiveness even more, and in any case, the internal damage has already occurred, so you are simply covering it up and sealing it in.

REBONDING ANTENNAS

The first step to rebonding is to remove the antenna. You might need someone else inside the aircraft to hold nuts for you. Be very careful when disconnecting the coaxial cable from the antenna; coax connectors can be very sensitive.

Blade antennas will have a gasket between the base of the antenna and the fuselage. Discard the gasket to ensure an excellent bond, or make sure there is a means of bonding the antenna to the airframe with the gasket in place.

Clean the metal base of the antenna with acetone to remove adhesive residue from the old gasket. Using a Scotchbrite pad, scuff the metal base until it's shiny and clean.

Apply some Alodine 1200 solution (wear rubber gloves while doing this), wait two to three minutes, and remove the excess by dabbing gently with a sponge, but don't rub it off. The Alodine is soft and can be easily scrubbed off. Make sure the contact area on the airplane's skin is cleaned and prepped also, using the same technique and the Alodine as you did with the antenna base.

Both com 1 and com 2 antennas are located on top of this Piper's fuselage. The aft antenna is located too close to the vertical stabilizer.

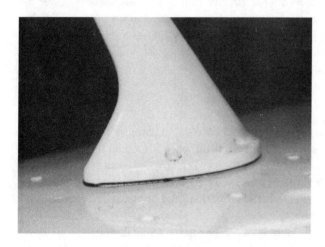

Com antenna. Note the gasket between the base of the antenna and the skin. It is recommended that the gasket be removed so the antenna can be RF-bonded to the skin unless there is positive bonding of the antenna with the gasket installed. Sealer can be installed around the base of the antenna to prevent water from getting into the antenna.

The gullwing antenna is a combined com 1 and dual nav antenna. The com 2 antenna is properly located about four feet aft of the front antenna.

Reinstall the antenna within 20 minutes. If the base of the antenna is provided with raised mating points, the only areas that need bonding are these points, which should contact the airplane skin solidly. Sometimes you have to use spacers to bond the antenna to a curved surface. If so, make sure the spacers are conductive and electrolytically compatible with both antenna and aircraft skin surfaces.

Composite airplanes and their control surfaces, gear doors, etc. are bonded essentially the same as metal airplanes. The key difference is the conductivity of the composite material. Graphite is somewhat conductive, whereas Fiberglas is totally nonconductive. In cases where the airframe is totally nonconductive, conductive paint is available and should be applied. In addition, a metal ground plane for antennas might have to be installed, either by embedding the ground plane underneath a thin layer of Fiberglas, or by installing it inside the composite skin if the skin isn't too thick. Don't ignore the necessity to install static wicks, also.

For a useful discussion of how to make concealed antennas for composite aircraft, contact Radio Systems Technology and order the *Antenna Reference Text*. RST also sells all the materials you'll need to build your own concealed antennas, plus parts to make transponder and DME antennas for composite airplanes. (See Sources for RST's address and phone number.)

8
Communication transmitters and receivers

MOST PILOTS PROBABLY THINK COM RADIOS—TRANSMITTERS AND receivers—are the most important avionics equipment in the aircraft. After all, when you first became a pilot, the very first radio you worked was most likely the com radio. If you're like most of us, you were probably nervous, worried that you weren't going to do it correctly and that if you didn't, your voice wouldn't be converted into electrical signals by the microphone, amplified in the com radio, and transmitted via the antenna to *anyone* on the same frequency.

Com radios are important. They are frequently your only contact with the outside world, especially when flying inside dank, gloomy clouds. Transmitters also use a lot more power than most avionics, and they are the first to go when you lose your alternator and end up draining the battery. It never ceases to amaze me how many "I learned about flying" stories you read where the pilot doesn't notice the alternator is dead until he starts to wonder why nobody seems to hear his transmissions anymore. Having a reliable communication system in your airplane makes your airplane more useful and provides a greater degree of mental and physical security.

KX 165 NAV/COMM with digital Radial

KX 165 NAV/COMM

NAV/COMM
Receiver &
transmitter (Back side)

KX 155 NAV/COMM

VOR
converter

Bendix/King navcom radios.

Glidescope receiver

The com transmitter amplifies the electrical signals from the microphone and delivers the amplified signals to the com antenna, where they are transmitted as radio waves. Aircraft com radios transmit amplitude modulated (AM) signals in the VHF range of the radio spectrum. Many people assume that because com radios transmit on frequencies from 118 to 136 MHz that the signals are FM, or frequency modulated, but that isn't the case. AM allows more frequencies to be used in a particular range of the spectrum, and if FM were used for com radios, we wouldn't be able to fit as many frequencies between 118 and 136 MHz. Also, although it provides better sound quality, FM is more complex and thus more expensive than AM. For ordinary voice transmission, we simply don't need the quality FM offers; we'd rather have the greater number of available frequencies and lower-quality audio.

The receiver amplifies the weak signals received at the antenna to the voice we hear on the headphones or speaker. You might have heard of the new frequency-tolerance standards that the FAA is requiring radios to meet. The new standard is 0.003 percent; previously the standard was 0.005 percent. Basically what the tolerance means is that a transmitter must transmit on the frequency selected within the tolerance standard. If the transmitter frequency drifts off beyond the tolerance limits, it could overlap and transmit on other nearby frequencies, causing no end of confusion in the aviation spectrum. With most radios using the full 720 channels allowed by 25-kHz frequency spacing, keeping transmitters within the allowable tolerance is even more important.

INSTALLATION TIPS

Modern, panel-mounted radios are highly sensitive and efficient. Mixing them, however, in a hybrid fashion, might not only cause cosmetic problems, but it could also create incompatibility problems, increasing installation and final checkout costs. I recommend settling on one brand for the whole avionics suite. If you can't afford the entire suite at once, have it installed piecemeal, with an eye towards ending up with a complete installation.

Selection of wire for the harness and coaxial cable for the antenna system is the responsibility of the shop doing the installation, but make sure the installers are using the highest-quality material. Careful attention to detail in the attachment of brackets, angles, fasteners, wiring harness assembly, RF and electrical bonding, and structural integrity will help you end up with a reliable avionics installation that will withstand rigorous use in the aeronautical environment.

If installing a new radio, I recommend using the antenna suggested by the radio manufacturer. A mismatched antenna and radio may result in reduced transmission and reception range.

If this is a retrofit radio, the older the wiring, the higher the possibility of damage from nicks, chafing, and cracking of insulation. Consider having new wiring installed, and new circuit breakers, too, as they deteriorate with age and could present a liability to the safe and reliable operation of the new radio.

ANTENNAS

The com antenna should be located perpendicular to the horizontal plane of the aircraft and at least 6 feet from DME and transponder antennas and 3 feet from ADF and other com antennas. The antenna should be kept clear of obstructions or projections such as the vertical stabilizer, landing gear doors, engines, and propellers. In some systems with dual coms, one antenna is mounted on the top of the fuselage, and the other, an angled wire antenna that runs vertically for about 10 inches then bends to run horizontally, is mounted on the belly. Other installations do fine with both com antennas mounted on top of the fuselage, provided there is enough room for the proper spacing. If one antenna is mounted on the belly, the landing gear doors must be bonded with a minimum of two braided straps at opposite ends of the doors to prevent blanking of transmission or reception while the gear doors are open and the airplane is on the ground.

Because some aluminum aircraft skins are too thin to support an antenna, your installer might have to add a reinforcement plate or doubler to the area where the antenna will be mounted to prevent cracking or tearing of the skin. If the skin is composite, a ground plane measuring at least 18 square inches will be required. If the composite skin is thicker than 90 thousands (0.090) of an inch, the ground plane will have to be installed externally on the skin and secured with fasteners or a layer of Fiberglas. Otherwise a dielectric effect could result, reducing antenna performance. See chapter 7 for more information on composite antenna installations.

COM RADIO PROBLEMS

Here is a useful flight-test routine to establish the performance of your communications radios:

1. First, review the manuals for your radios to make sure you're completely familiar with how they operate and what kind of performance to expect from them.

2. Before takeoff, operate all flight controls through their full range of travel to assure there is no interference in your radios. Ask for a radio check on both com 1 and com 2 while constantly listening for static, breakup, and blanketing effects of reception and transmission. Turn on rotating beacons, operate flaps, cowl flaps, and other flight controls while operating the radios.

3. Listen for ignition noise and interference from other electrical equipment and the effect communications have on the navigation radios. Confirm that the communications radios are clear of extraneous noise and that your transmissions and receptions on the radio test are loud and clear, without background static. If everything checks okay on the ground, take the airplane up for a flight test.

4. After takeoff, try to contact a facility that is 50 nautical miles away. If your transmitter has a high and low power setting, try the radio check on both settings. Try transmitting and receiving while in a 10-degree bank and make sure you don't lose contact while in the turn.

5. Operate the squelch control and determine if it functions properly and doesn't cause any adverse effects.

6. Try the same radio check test at a distance of 30 miles; the facility you are talking to should hear you loud and clear. If not, continue towards the facility until they can hear you loud and clear and note the distance you are from that facility.

7. Ask for a practice approach at a tower-controlled airport. Put the airplane into approach configuration as though you were going to land. You should have the gear and flaps down, all radios set for the appropriate approach, marker beacon audio on, ADF tracking the LOM if there is one. During the approach, observe and listen for noise in the audio, abnormal needle fluctuations in the nav radios, and any other abnormal indications.

8. Note that these tests are much easier and safer if you bring another pilot along to help fly or watch for traffic while you test the radios.

These procedures are designed to evaluate communications quality during turns, approaches, landing configuration, and at a distance from the ground facility. Any loss of radio contact in a particular radial bearing from the ground facility could be due to unequal torquing of the antenna base to the airframe, poor bonding, a defective antenna, or airframe obstructions (vertical stabilizer, landing gear, flaps, etc.). Confirmation of these problems will help lead you towards a solution—not always an inexpensive solution, but a solution nevertheless.

TROUBLESHOOTING TIPS

Keep in mind that if you have dual coms, audio and microphone selection is likely selected through a common audio panel. In most such installations, audio is also amplified as it passes through the audio panel. This common element can help you isolate the cause of a problem.

If your installation has dual coms of the same brand and type, one of the easiest ways to isolate com problems is to switch radios. That way you can isolate whether the problem is in the radio or in the airplane. If it's in the radio, then you don't need to bring the airplane to the avionics shop.

Don't try removing any radios unless you've been shown specifically how to do it. Each manufacturer has its own special method of locking radios into the panel, and while it might seem simple, there is usually a trick to doing it right and a special tool. If you are not a licensed airframe mechanic, you are not allowed to remove and install your radios, unless you are doing so under the supervision of a licensed mechanic. Don't forget that FAR Part 43 requires that all maintenance performed be signed off in the logbooks, so make sure the A&P you are working with signs off each time the radios are removed, installed, and switched. This will also help you keep track of problems and their resolution. Unfortunately, many shops ignore the requirement to sign the logbooks when radios are removed and reinstalled for repair, but the requirement is there. It's just a matter of you insisting that it be done in order to maintain the documentation integrity of your airplane.

Frequently you can clear up a transmission or reception problem by removing, cleaning, and reinstalling a radio. You can clean the flat, metal contacts on the back of the radio by gently scrubbing the metal with a clean pencil eraser. Be careful not to remove any metal from the contacts.

The following paragraphs name some symptoms and suggestions for the cause.

Receiver doesn't work. Check to see if the microphone is keyed. The easiest way to rule this out is to replace the mic with a known good mic. Also check that the radio and audio panel are properly seated in their trays. Is this problem occurring on both radios or just one? Don't forget to check whether the circuit breaker has popped out or the fuse hasn't blown (if it uses fuses instead of circuit breakers). There could also be an antenna or coaxial cable problem.

Garbled reception, breaking up. Check for a misaligned receiver (where the frequency is slightly off tolerance) or poor shielding. Also check for receiver gain set too high, mic gain set too high, or a defective intercom. If you have an intercom, turn it off, or if it can't be shut off, try using the emergency/spare mic jack.

Com won't transmit. The mic key button could be defective. Again, try another good mic. Also check contacts on mic jack. Is the jack making proper contact? (See chapter 5.) Check circuit breaker or fuse. Is the radio fully seated in its tray? Also check audio panel seating. Is the audio panel correctly set to transmit on the radio you're using? There could also be an antenna or coaxial cable problem.

Tower says they can hear carrier wave only, but not voice. This could be from a broken wire in the mic. Try a new mic, and if that works, examine the old mic to see if it's just a broken wire that can be easily fixed (see chapter 5).

Intermittent transmission. Try a backup mic. It could also be a defective relay in the com radio or antenna problems.

Transmission squawked as weak, garbled, breaking up, or noisy. Try backup mic. Also make sure your lips are close enough to the mic. If it's not the mic, it could be a misaligned transmitter or faulty antenna system or coaxial cable problem.

Headsets are not working. Try using copilot's jacks or another headset to see if the problem is in the airplane or the headset.

Speaker inoperative. Try the headset to make sure the audio system is working. (Don't forget to set the audio panel correctly to listen on headphones.) If system works with headsets, the problem could be a defective speaker, wiring, or amplifier.

COM AND NAVCOM MANUFACTURERS

The following lists several recommended communications and navigation/communications radios.

Aire-Sciences

Becker Avionics

Bendix/King

Collins Avionics

Icom

ICS (available from Wag Aero)

McCoy Avionics (replacement front end for older King radios)

Narco Avionics

S-TEC

Sigma-Tek

Radio Systems Technology (available as kit or factory built)

Terra Avionics

TKM Michel (slide-in replacements for older King, Narco, and ARC radios)

Val Avionics

HAND-HELD TRANSCEIVER MANUFACTURERS

These companies offer handheld transceivers. See Sources for addresses.

Bendix/King

Communications Specialists

Icom

McCoy Avionics

Narco Avionics

Sporty's Pilot Shop

Terra Avionics

9
Navigation receivers

YOUR VOR SYSTEM IS PRIMARILY DESIGNED TO RECEIVE SIGNALS THAT will feed information to drive a needle or other form of steering display, referred to as a *course deviation indicator*. These systems consist of the receiver, indicator, antenna system, and in the case of remote black boxes, frequency-channeling control heads. All of the systems drive an indicator, whether it is a separate omni head in your instrument panel or an LCD display in the panel-mounted radio, like Bendix/King's new KX125 navcom.

Nav receivers operate on frequencies between 108.00 to 117.95 MHz. VOR frequencies are the even tenths (110.3, for example) and ILS uses the odds (109.35, for example). This is important to know because ILS frequencies will not work if the frequency common (ground) is missing, while the VOR will work fine. The opposite is true if the ILS common circuit is always grounded; then the VOR frequencies won't work. In other words, to ensure that the VOR is switched off when you are using the ILS frequencies, the ILS common wire is grounded when you tune in an ILS frequency. When you tune in a VOR frequency, the ILS common is ungrounded so only the VOR frequencies will work.

Bendix/King com and KNS80 RNAV system.

INSTALLATION TIPS

As with any radio installation, proper assembly of the wiring harness and use of high-quality wiring is a critical step. If this is a retrofit, consider replacing the old wiring and circuit breakers at the same time to prevent reliability problems.

Standard RG-58 coaxial cable is usually used for the antenna system, but when electromagnetic interference is a potential problem, double-shielded cable might be necessary. Most installations use one nav antenna and a coupler to tie together the two pieces of coax cable from the individual nav receivers. If you can afford it and there is enough room for two antennas, it would be best to install two nav antennas and separate coax cables for each nav receiver.

NAV ANTENNAS

There are two nav antennas in common use today: the V-shaped dipole, which looks like two pieces of thick wire mounted on the top of your airplane's vertical fin, and the balanced-loop antenna. The V-shaped dipole tends to be more "blind" to reception of signals to the side or perpendicular to the aircraft's flight path. As the airplane approaches a VOR station, the signal will be stable, but as the airplane passes by the VOR, the nav CDI needle will become nervous. Because terrain obstructions such as buildings or mountains can twist the normally horizontally polarized VOR signals (see chapter 7), two signals could result, and the dipole antenna will receive both signals and display this as an error (a jerky or erratic needle). The balanced-loop antenna will reject these unwanted signals, whereas the dipole will not.

The balanced-loop antenna comes in two designs: the towel bar, which mounts on a vertical surface like the vertical stabilizer, or the blade, which looks like a normal knife-shaped blade antenna.

The decision to replace a dipole antenna with a balanced-loop antenna could become more pressing when you are having RNAV installed. RNAV systems require antennas that are capable of receiving signals from all directions, because RNAV works off VORs that are not necessarily in the line of flight. You can try testing a new RNAV with the old antenna by flight-testing the RNAV system using raw VOR data without turning on the RNAV functions and looking for errors while in this mode. If none are detected, the odds are that the system should work okay without installing a balanced-loop antenna, but isn't it worth the time and effort to simply install the best antenna in the first place? The initial higher cost of the antenna and installation will eventually be outweighed by the savings in squawks incurred during the system's lifetime.

Replacement of the dipole antenna with a balanced loop will increase nav range by a considerable amount, up to 25 percent, even when on the ground. Also, if you fly in icing conditions, the blade or towel bar antenna is more resistant to icing damage and won't break off as easily as the wire dipole.

VOR PROBLEMS

If your airplane has dual VOR receivers, take advantage of having both by comparing one to the other during troubleshooting. You can switch receivers and/or indicators to isolate the problem as well.

Just as with com systems, initial troubleshooting begins with listening to the audio, in this case the VOR or ILS or localizer identifier. The audio you hear is carried on the same signal that drives the CDI. Therefore, if the CDI isn't working and you can hear the station identifier, the problem is either in the converter, interconnect wiring, or the indicator.

Select a station with a strong audio signal to confirm the frequency you selected. Everything needed for the converter to drive the left/right needle is converted from that signal. Listen carefully for noise. Any noise detected within that audio will tend to override or drown out the signal, in essence producing a relatively weak signal. What you'll see on the indicator is erratic needles. If the audio is loud and clear but the indicator doesn't work at all, the problem is most likely within the converter, which is located either in the receiver or inside the indicator. Obviously, a qualified shop will have to perform repairs to fix this problem.

If the audio is noisy in both receivers, the problem can be isolated to a common system: the antennas. The problem can be anything from a defective antenna to poor RF bonding to broken or kinked coaxial cables. If the VOR is working but the localizer isn't, it's possible that the common wire for the ILS frequencies has broken, which would prevent the localizer from channeling. This wire should be grounded when the localizer frequency is selected but should not read to ground when a VOR frequency is selected.

When testing your VOR system, if you have RNAV, make sure it's set to allow normal VOR operation so you don't try and troubleshoot something that is simply the result of a switch setting.

One area that could cause a problem is the nav coaxial cables. I've seen it happen where the nav and com cables get switched, accidentally of course. Although the com and nav systems can still operate, they won't be as efficient and could cause you to spend money trying to track down the problem elsewhere.

Proper installation of radios in their racks is a primary concern when beginning troubleshooting. Many times radios are removed and incorrectly reinstalled so that the rear connector is not seating properly with the rack's rear mating connector. Another possibility is that during original installation, the radio rack was located too far back from the front of the instrument panel, not allowing the connectors to make solid contact. You can check this by measuring from the back of the radio bezel (the radio's faceplate) to the rear of the radio. Take another measurement from the front of the instrument panel to the connector in the back of the radio rack. Compare the two measurements. Do they indicate there is a compatible relationship between the radio plug and its mating connector? The difference doesn't have to be much to break contact or cause intermittent contact, especially on ribbon connectors or F-style contacts.

F-style contacts are a terminal created from flat metal stock and rolled into a circular form, except for the crimp section. The crimp section is left open; a side view gives the appearance of the letter "F." The conductor crimp is the short portion of the "F," while the longer section or insulation crimp is the upper part of the "F." These F-style contacts are used in many avionics installations, especially panel-mounted radios. A small tab acts to retain the terminal in the connector block. After a lot of use, this tab wears out the plastic housing and the tab can pop out. Other failure points are the spring-loading of the contact against the mating connector. Eventually, after much use, the spring-loading tension deteriorates and must be readjusted, or the contact must be replaced.

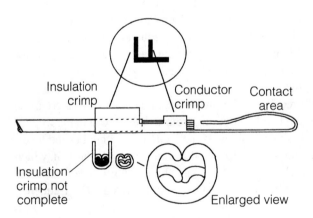

Insulation crimp   Conductor crimp   Contact area

Insulation crimp not complete   Enlarged view

"F" style terminal; found in many panel-mounted radio stacks.

If you have two nav receivers and both are displaying similar indications, such as weak or erratic reception, it is likely that there is an antenna system (coaxial cable, couplers, connectors, or antennas) problem or that there is a bonding problem at the antennas or on control surfaces. To test this, your avionics shop can test your system without taking the airplane apart using a test set. They'll situate the test antenna about 12 inches from the nav antenna on the right side of the vertical stabilizer and radiate a 60- to 70-dB signal, slowly decreasing the dB level until the nav flag pulls and the CDI needle swings. They'll do the same for the left side of the antenna and compare the readings. With a balanced-loop antenna system, found on most light-aircraft nav systems, the readings where the flag pulls and swings the needle should be virtually the same. Any variation of more than 4 to 6 dB indicates a problem with the antenna. In this case, you'd want to change the entire antenna, including the coupler and the short cables between the antenna and coupler.

Here is a simple ground check you can perform yourself. With the nav radios on and tuned to a nearby station (obviously you need to be at an airport where you can tune in a local VOR to do this test), have a partner take a long broom handle and tap gently on the antenna elements. Watch the CDIs and listen to the audio for any increase in noise or needle movement. This could indicate a defective antenna or coaxial cable connections. Move the control surfaces while watching the CDIs and listening to the nav audio. You shouldn't see any needle movement or hear any noise while the control surfaces are moving.

The easiest way to rule out or confirm a coaxial cable problem is to bypass the existing cable with a length of known, good cable, then test the system using the existing antennas. If this test shows there is a definite coax problem, before replacing the entire length of coax in the airplane, check for bad bulkhead fittings, where the coax is split and connected with connectors to go through a bulkhead. It would be much easier to replace a bad connector or two than to replace the entire length of coaxial cable. If you're lucky, you might find that during manufacture, extra lengths of coax were laid in the airplane, and you might be able to make use of one of these pieces of coax, saving you a lot of time and effort.

VOR GROUND CHECK

If you fly IFR, you must have logged a VOR test within the past 30 days. There are two ways to do the test on the ground. One is to use an FAA VOR test facility (VOT) or a radiated test signal from your avionics shop's equipment. Note that if having the check done by your avionics shop, the test must be logged by the shop itself because it's their equipment that is providing the signal. The VOT is like a VOR that broadcasts only one radial. Perform the check by tuning in the VOT frequency and centering the CDI. With a "from" flag showing, the OBS should read 0 degrees. With a "to" flag showing, the OBS should read 180 degrees. At the same time, you should be able to receive the audio from the VOT facility. Maximum error on this test is 4 degrees.

The other VOR ground check method is a VOR checkpoint on the ground if your airport has one designated. If you have dual navs installed in your airplane, you can check one against the other using the VOR ground check point. The maximum permissible error between the two navs is 4 degrees.

NAV FLIGHT TEST

You can perform the VOR test in the air using certified airborne checkpoints. In this case, the maximum error is 6 degrees.

Here is another useful test: fly over a landmark at a right angle (90 degrees) to a VOR within good reception range. Center the needle when you're exactly 90 degrees to the VOR. Note your position relative to a good landmark below you. Turn the airplane around and, leaving the nav radio alone, check the needle when you fly over the same landmark in the opposite direction but still 90 degrees to the VOR. The needle should still be centered. If not, this might be an indication of a nav antenna that's not sensitive to all azimuths. Before replacing the antenna, try rebonding it and equally torque its fasteners; then perform the test again.

If your antenna is the inexpensive V-shaped rabbit-ear dipole, you might want to consider upgrading to the more efficient and reliable towel-bar or blade-type balanced-loop antenna. The balanced-loop antenna has a broader directional reception. On the other hand, the V-shaped dipole antenna is most effective in the open section of the V, which is directly behind the airplane.

An important note: while your nav radios might be within limits on the VOR test, don't assume that means they are working perfectly. As you fly toward the range limit of the nav radios, any error will be magnified. At the maximum reception range for a VOR, for instance, the error could be unacceptably high due to the weaker signals at that distance. If you rely heavily on your nav radios for IFR flying, consider having them recalibrated by your avionics shop once a year to prevent the loss of accuracy as signal strength diminishes. Locations and frequencies of certified VOTs and ground and airborne test points are listed in the FAA's *Airport/Facility Directory*.

AREA NAVIGATION

This discussion of RNAV is limited because it is becoming somewhat of a dinosaur with the advent of sophisticated new loran and GPS sets. RNAV is still useful because its use is fully integrated into the current ATC system, but its high price makes it nearly as expensive as an IFR loran, and the loran can do a lot more for your money. GPS IFR approaches look like a certainty in the not-too-distant future, so in comparing RNAV to GPS, both in terms of price and features, GPS wins hands down.

What follows is a ramp checklist, courtesy of Bendix/King, for testing RNAV system accuracy. This test allows you to perform a simple ground test, eliminating the need to have a shop drag out their expensive equipment. Most shops use this test anyway.

Before beginning this test, make sure strong DME and VOR signals are available and that they both work with the RNAV set to VOR mode (both DME and VOR signals are necessary for operation of RNAV systems).

Test 1

1. Select VOR mode on RNAV.

2. Record radial to VOR station by centering CDI with "to" indication.

3. Set up an RNAV waypoint using a radial 90 degrees greater than the radial showing on the CDI.

4. Set the waypoint distance equal to the DME distance indicated to the VOR.

5. Select RNAV enroute mode.

6. Rotate the OBS until the CDI centers with a "to" flag.

7. RNAV distance should read 1.41 times DME distance (plus or minus five nautical miles) and indicated course should be 45 degrees (plus or minus 2 degrees) greater than the VOR radial recorded in step 2.

Test 2

1. Select VOR mode on RNAV.

2. Record radial to VOR station by centering CDI with "to" indication.

3. Program a waypoint with a radial 120 degrees greater than the indicated VOR radial.

4. Program the waypoint distance equal to the indicated DME distance.

5. Select RNAV enroute mode.

6. Rotate the OBS until the CDI centers with a "to" flag.

7. RNAV distance should equal DME distance (plus or minus five nautical miles) and indicated course should be 60 degrees greater than the VOR radial recorded in step b.

GLIDESLOPE RECEIVERS

Because glideslope receivers are usually built into the nav box, failure of the glideslope might be a fault of the nav receiver. Obviously you would notice if the nav failed and make the correct assumption that the glideslope is also inoperative before trying to use it on an approach. The glideslope is fairly simple in design and layout, so if it has failed, it shouldn't be that difficult for your avionics shop to fix. Typically, more problems are caused by shielding integrity, bonding, and proper installation than simple wiring failure.

Other transmitters can easily affect the sensitive glideslope receiver, so make sure all antenna connections are secure and that there is sufficient distance between antennas (2 to 3 feet minimum).

Some systems interface the nav and glideslope to the nav antenna with a coupler. If the nav is working but the glideslope isn't, check the coupler to the glideslope receiver. It's possible that the coaxial cable was disconnected during maintenance, say when the nose cone was removed, or the center conductor was pulled out of the coax connector.

On single-engine airplanes where the factory or the installer has placed the glideslope antenna just inside the windshield, you might see a problem with the glideslope needle wavering slightly up and down from propeller modulation. Except for confirming that the receiver is fine, the coaxial cable is intact, and the antenna is in good shape, there isn't much you can do about prop modulation. You might try changing the coaxial cable or the antenna. A better solution would be to install an external glideslope antenna away from the propeller's effects, or tie the glideslope receiver to the nav antenna with a coupler.

NAV RECEIVER MANUFACTURERS

These navigation receiver manufacturer's addresses can be found in the Sources section at the end of this book.

Aire-Sciences

Becker Avionics

Bendix/King

Collins Avionics

ICS Plus (available from Wag Aero)

Narco Avionics

Radio Systems Technology (available as kit or factory built)

S-TEC

Sigma-Tek

Terra Avionics

TKM Michel

10
Marker beacons

MARKER BEACONS ARE ONE OF THE SIMPLEST PIECES OF AVIONICS equipment in your airplane. One of three lights and a distinctive audio tone notify you that you're flying over a marker transmitter. The marker display is usually included in the audio panel, although you can buy it separately. The entire system consists of an antenna, coaxial cable, audio circuits, a receiver, and a switch or two.

The white marker light is for the inner and airway marker; you'll rarely see this one light up. It is activated by a 3000-Hz tone from the transmitter. The middle marker emits a 1300-Hz tone and lights the amber light on the panel and is found about 3,500 feet from the end of the runway. The outer marker is a 400-Hz tone that lights the blue lamp on your panel at the point where you normally intersect the glideslope and begin descending, 4 to 7 miles from the end of the runway.

Marker systems are very sensitive to long cable runs or poor antenna location, especially if the antenna is being shadowed by other antennas or obstructions.

INSTALLATION TIPS

The antenna should be located near the front of the aircraft, with the coaxial cable as short as possible to reduce signal loss to the receiver. Although engineers like to have the antenna as close to the receiver as possible, the design of the antenna and the fact that marker transmitters are directly underneath the airplane when the signals are received dictates that the antenna be installed on the aircraft's belly, preferably no further aft than where the belly turns upwards toward the tailcone.

Marker beacon receiver mounted in a Cessna single, located on sidewall below instrument panel on copilot's side.

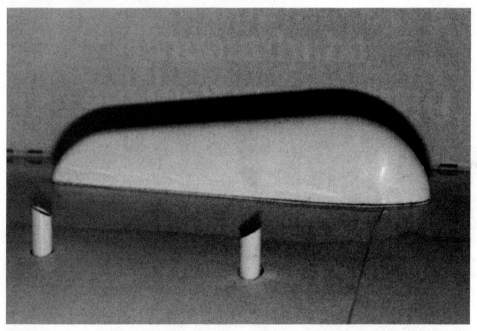

Boat-style marker beacon antenna.

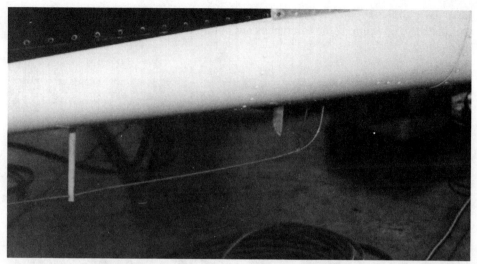

Towel-bar-style marker beacon antenna, a common source of many marker beacon squawks. Replacement with boat-style antenna is strongly recommended.

The antenna is usually a long blade or boat-style, but you'll also see the older-style (cheaper), thin, towel-rack type rod with a sliding adjustment.

MARKER PROBLEMS

Failures associated with the marker beacon system are usually related to broken wires, failed antenna systems, burned-out bulbs, or receiver degradation due to age and vibration. You've probably noticed that the blue light is difficult to see, even under normal lighting conditions, but especially when the sun is shining on the panel. To get used to what the light looks like, shadow the light with your hand while you check it with the test switch.

Don't forget to set the sensitivity switch to the "high" position when checking marker beacons in the air and during instrument approaches. You wouldn't want to squawk a market reception problem that is caused by simple incorrect positioning of the switches. By the same token, whenever flying VFR and especially if your airplane is flown by VFR pilots who don't know how to use the marker beacons, make sure the marker audio is switched off. One accident happened to a student pilot who panicked when the marker started flashing and beeping at him as he flew over the marker transmitter. The student thought something serious was wrong with the airplane and performed a not-so-flawless emergency landing.

Vibration eventually causes the center contact on the bulb to wear out where it touches the spring-loaded contact in the socket. Replace the bulb when this happens.

When the antenna starts to deteriorate, the first light to lose its brilliancy is the blue outer marker. Cause of the problem could be a bad antenna or simply poor bonding. Weak reception might be nothing more than factory tolerances having slipped. First have the avionics shop bench check the receiver, then test the system in the airplane to isolate the problem. If the tolerances are not up to spec, the shop will adjust them as required.

Close view of towel-bar marker beacon antenna where it mounts on belly of airplane. Note the corrosion, which should be removed prior to antenna rebonding or replacement.

During testing, it's nearly impossible to activate the marker receiver with the test equipment antenna inside the cockpit. Except for direct coupling tests, the technician will usually have to place the test antenna within 12 inches of the marker antenna on the belly. If the tech has to place the test antenna closer than 12 inches to activate the marker beacon receiver, it could indicate that the receiver's switches are set to "low" sensitivity, a defective or weak antenna, shorted coaxial cable, an open circuit in the receiver, or receiver needing calibration.

If the receiver tests okay, have the antenna rebonded or do it yourself (see chapter 7). If antenna rebonding doesn't help, replace the antenna and coaxial cable. In most cases of marker problems I've worked on, the antenna was the problem, especially when it was the old-style towel-rack antenna previously mentioned.

MARKER BEACON RECEIVER MANUFACTURERS

These companies manufacture marker beacon receivers. See their addresses in the Sources section of this book.

Bendix/King

Collins Avionics

Narco Avionics

Radio Systems Technology (available in kit form or factory built)

Sigma-Tek

Terra Avionics

11
Automatic direction finders

THE AUTOMATIC DIRECTION FINDER (ADF) MIGHT SEEM AN ANACHRONISM in these days of ultra-precise GPS and reasonably precise loran systems, but ADF is still a useful, simple, and widely used navigation system. Fancy nav systems get all the glory, but ADF is frequently the nav system of last resort for Alaska bush pilots and over-water ferry pilots. ADF is still the nav system of only resort, with the exception of GPS, in the former Soviet Union.

The frequencies transmitted by the nondirectional beacons (NDBs) that drive your ADF needle are in the low-frequency range of the radio spectrum, 190 to 1750 kHz, which happens to include the same frequencies used by commercial AM broadcast stations. Your ADF will not only receive the commercial stations' audio signal but can home in on their powerful signals as well, providing you with a backup means of verifying your position or course, if you know the frequency of the broadcast station and where its antenna is located. Remember, however, that you can't use these commercial stations for primary navigation.

Be careful about using commercial stations at night, because the higher frequencies they use tend to bounce off the atmosphere and not hug the ground. The signals received by your ADF should be ground waves that hug the ground, which the lower frequencies tend to do, even at night. Sky waves that bounce off the atmosphere are not accurate because they don't always bounce straight.

KR 87 Digital ADF with Standby frequency (actual size)

"Flip-flop" of Active and Standby frequencies

Flight Time display

Elapsed Time display

The KR 87 System:
KA 44 Combined Loop & Sense Antenna
KI 227 Indicator
KR 87 Ditigal ADF

Bendix/King KR87 ADF system.

Because the ADF can always get some audio signal, many technicians find it useful as a troubleshooting aid for checking audio quality and output. This way, the tech doesn't have to be constantly calling the tower or someone in the shop on a test frequency for radio checks.

Another use for the ADF is finding the locater outer marker (LOM) on IFR approaches. You get double confirmation when you fly over: a flashing blue light and audio tone from the marker beacon, and reversal of the ADF needle.

Many pilots have found the ADF useful in determining the location of thunderstorms. Using an off-station frequency where the needle simply goes in circles because there is no human-generated signal, you can sometimes watch the needle point in the direction of the huge electrical discharges produced by lightning. If you have the ADF audio turned on, you can hear these discharges as well; they sound like loud scratchy waves.

ADFs are susceptible to interference from varying weather conditions, time of day, and even geographic location, so keep these effects in mind when troubleshooting ADF problems.

FRONT END FOR KING ADF

McCoy Avionics makes a digital-display, multiple-memory front end replacement for Bendix/King's KR85 ADF. The MAC 1850 front end includes storage for 10 ADF frequencies, a countdown/up timer that has a vocal callout feature so you can listen to the timer countdown on an IFR approach while you concentrate on flying the airplane, and other useful features.

When considering this kind of upgrade to your ADF, don't forget that the new front end is only going to make the radio as good as the radio's guts. If the radio isn't in good shape already, then adding this front end won't make it any better.

INSTALLATION TIPS

Ask your avionics shop if they will include in your price any adjustments that need to be made to ensure accuracy of your ADF system after it's installed. This applies particularly to quadrantal error described later in this chapter.

ADFs are particularly sensitive to extraneous noise, and correct routing of the ADF's wiring is critical to avoid noise problems. Normally standard RG-58 coaxial cable is satisfactory, but double or triple shielded coax made by manufacturers such as Belden, Times, or Essex is recommended. All harness wiring should not be routed parallel to or in close proximity to DME wiring, transponder wiring, and power-carrying wires, especially those from the alternator. All necessary wire crossover should be executed at right angles to reduce the possible induction of unwanted noise.

ANTENNAS

ADF antennas have evolved considerably, from the old loop antenna that actually rotated to the modern combined loop and sense antenna in one streamlined unit. If you're replacing an ADF and your airplane has the less-than-modern wire-sense antenna that goes from the tail to the top of the fuselage and the loop antenna on the belly, now is the time to upgrade to the combined loop and sense antenna. It works a lot better and is much easier to maintain.

The ADF antenna should be mounted 4 to 6 feet from DME antennas and at least 3 feet from com antennas. It should be kept clear of obstructions or projections such as the vertical stabilizer, landing gear doors, engines and propellers. Any openings such as access panels will break the smooth ground plane required by the antenna, so keep the antenna as far away as possible from access panels. If this isn't possible, make sure the access panels are well bonded (electrically) to the airframe.

Installing the combined loop/sense antenna on the belly or top of the fuselage won't make any difference when the airplane is flying. The belly location, however, will reduce signal quality on the ground. If installing the antenna on a low-wing airplane, the antenna should be mounted aft of the wing. Some loop/sense antennas, like Bendix/King's, have drain holes. If mounting the antenna on top of the fuselage, plug the drain hole with silicone sealant.

As usual, if the mounting point isn't strong enough to accept an antenna by itself, the installer might have to add an aluminum doubler to the area before mounting the antenna. The doubler must be RF bonded to the airframe.

ADF PROBLEMS

The best way to operationally check an ADF receiver is to select a strong commercial frequency and check for correct needle pointing. If the needle points to the station correctly, select the NDB frequency on which the ADF was squawked as giving poor performance. Assuming the higher-strength commercial station works and the lower power NDB doesn't, the problem might be a defective antenna system or defective receiver. Have the receiver bench-checked before tearing into the antenna system.

A short-circuited antenna, failure of the RF section of the receiver, or defective wiring interconnect can cause weak reception. If you suspect any of these problems, have the receiver bench-checked. Of course, other problems such as obstructions between the aircraft and the station, onboard noise caused by other equipment, and ambient weather conditions can also limit ADF reception. Being a low-frequency signal, reception of NDB signals is much more sensitive to atmospheric conditions than the higher-frequency VHF signals used for communications and VOR navigation.

If the pointer doesn't point to the station at all, the problem might be wiring or equipment failure. Either problem can cause the same symptom, requiring isolation of the problem by point-to-point checking of wiring and bench checking of the ADF unit. Don't ignore the possibility that the NDB might have been out of commission for the time during which the ADF didn't work on that station.

The alternator can be a big source of ADF interference and can wipe out several frequencies or even just the lower band of frequencies. If the ADF displays signs of failure with the engine running but works fine with the engine off, try shutting off the alternator switch while the engine is running and see if that makes a difference in the reception. To perform this test, shut off all radios and electrical equipment before shutting off the alternator. Then shut off the alternator, if you have a switch to do so. If not, you might have to pull the alternator field circuit breaker to take it off line. Turn the

ADF back on and note whether the ADF reception improves with the alternator off. Before you turn the alternator on again, make sure the ADF and all other electrical equipment is off first. Turning the alternator on and off can create an electrical surge that could damage sensitive equipment, especially avionics.

Noise from other sources such as the DME and transponder can affect ADF operation. Some DMEs, such as the one that is part of older versions of King's KNS80 RNAV, lack a modification that prevents noise being injected into the ADF receiver. You can check for interference from the DME and transponder by checking ADF operation with DME and transponder on and off, or both on and both off. If you suspect either one is causing a problem, talk it over with your avionics tech and ask if there are any modifications that should be done to the offending radio to prevent this problem. If the ADF needle rotates continuously and doesn't point at the station, check for breaks in the sense antenna (the long wire antenna from the vertical stabilizer to the top of the fuselage, on airplanes where the sense and loop antenna aren't combined in one unit).

Check for missing audio by setting the switch on the ADF box to the ANT (or antenna) position. Missing audio may be traced to the loop antenna or the receiver. Being on the airplane's belly, the loop antenna is susceptible to oil and water contamination, especially when the airplane is being washed, causing water to find its way into the mating connector. Narco antennas have a built-in cup that will hold quite a bit of water and still allow the antenna to work for a while, but not very well. Cleaning the water off and reassembling the connector might help, but possibly only temporarily because damage could already have been done. Narco provides a sealer kit to prevent moisture entry, so if this isn't installed on your Narco antenna, you might want to have it done.

Troubleshooting ADF problems can be tricky because there are so many factors that can affect the ADF. You have the responsibility of communicating with the technician to help them do their job efficiently and accurately. You are a critical part of the troubleshooting link. Let the technician know the time of day, type of weather, altitude, speed, and what other equipment was on when the problem showed up. When the malfunction occurs, try to shut down other pieces of equipment to see if you can isolate the problem to a specific system that is interfering with the ADF.

ADF SYSTEM OPERATIONAL CHECK

Here is a checklist for operationally checking your ADF system. This should be done after a new ADF installation and after any repairs.

1. Check all power and ground connections before turning on power.
2. Turn on power and turn on the ADF. Listen to the ADF audio in both the ANT or antenna position and the ADF position. In the ADF position, the receiver should function as a directional finder, pointing toward a known, good station. ANT or antenna position allows the radio to operate only as an audio receiver. I recommend identifying the station with the switch in the ANT or antenna position first then switching to ADF mode.

3. Once you switch to ADF mode, the needle should point directly to the station. During daylight hours, you'll have to perform a flight test to get an accurate test of the system. There are two types of errors you need to check for: constant and quadrantal. A *constant* error is the difference between the correct bearing and that which is displayed on the indicator. Fixing a constant error might only require adjustment of the receiver. Antenna adjustment might be possible, but the antenna will have to be removed to make the adjustment. After realigning the ADF, select an NDB station with a known magnetic heading from your position. Your ADF needle should point to that heading, indicating a relative bearing of plus or minus 3 degrees.

   Quadrantal error isn't constant and usually varies in each 90-degree quadrant and is dependent on the receiver quality and location of the loop antenna. Some receivers allow for fine calibration to remove quadrantal error, and it could take many test flights to make these adjustments.

4. While still in flight, switch between the ADF and ANT positions, ending up with the switch in the ADF position. Did the needle move, without sluggishness, directly to the station? Make sure the needle isn't reversing (pointing opposite to where the station is).

5. If a compass card is connected to your ADF system, make sure the card follows within two degrees of the ADF needle when you turn.

6. Turn all other avionics off and check if the audio is clear of extraneous noise caused by nonavionics electrical equipment like strobes or electrical actuators, etc.

7. Turn other avionics systems on one at a time and check for noise and interference problems. If you find a problem, you need to check into why that system is suddenly causing an interference problem with your ADF. It could be that another system has had a problem all along and you just didn't notice it until you had the ADF installed. Any time alternators, generators, strobes, electrical actuators, and control surfaces are replaced, make sure all bonds and filters are reinstalled and are in good shape.

8. If you've had a new autopilot installed recently, check the ADF with the autopilot turned on, engaged, and tracking a nearby VOR or the heading bug. Listen to the ADF audio and watch the needle. Now turn the autopilot off. Was there any change? Did the ADF audio improve or the needle swing to a new heading? If it's a Century autopilot, the autopilot's 5-kHz oscillator (in the autopilot amplifier) might be generating interference through the common bus, the grounding system, or by radiation. For this type of interference problem, it is especially important that the ADF antennas, the receiver, and all grounds adequately bonded to the airframe before attempting any other fixes. Why? Until the autopilot was installed, there wasn't an interference problem. With the new autopilot, however, the ADF is particularly sensitive to signals in the frequency range of noise and the autopilot's 5-kHz generator.

The answer to this problem also might be relocation of components, either the autopilot or the ADF. Or the problem could be solved by relocating harnesses, making sure power lines are shielded, or installing filters in the power lines at the source of the noise, or if impractical, at the receiver of the noise. Another possibility is to lift the autopilot's amplifier off of the ground, eliminating the contact and conduit between the noise generator and the aircraft's chassis.

If nothing else works, try relocating the ADF antenna.

One other slim possibility is that the noise is getting in through wire shielding. This is called a *parasitic oscillation* or *ground loop*, and it can occur in cable shielding, even with both ends grounded. To isolate this, lift the shields from ground, one at a time, until the problem goes away.

After reading this, it might appear that this is nothing more than a shotgun approach, trying everything until it finally works. With some problems, it could be that a shotgun approach is the only method that will finally solve the problem, but usually the rebonding, grounding, bus isolation, and antenna relocation can resolve the problem. However, note that these measures should have been done during installation.

ADF MANUFACTURERS

These manufacturers offer ADF receivers. Their addresses are in the Sources section of this book.

Becker Avionics

Bendix/King

Collins Avionics

McCoy Avionics (front end replacement for Bendix/King KR85)

Narco Avionics

S-TEC

Sigma-Tek

Terra Avionics

12
Distance-measuring equipment

DISTANCE-MEASURING EQUIPMENT (DME) IS DERIVED FROM THE MILITARY tactical air navigation (TACAN) system. Where TACAN provides both distance and navigation bearing, DME displays the actual slant range distance (within 0.1 percent) from the aircraft to the station. Slant range means that the distance measured is directly from the aircraft to the station, so that if you are flying 5000 feet above a DME station, your DME will show that you are one mile from that station. Until the advent of GPS, DME has been the only truly accurate distance-measuring type equipment available to light aircraft.

DME uses highly accurate measurement of a UHF (ultra-high frequency) pulse transmission to determine distance to a ground station. The on-board transmitter sends a pulse to the ground station and receives a pulse in return. The aircraft's unit computes the time delay between the two pulses and converts it into a distance, time, or speed display on the DME face. Because of the DME's precision, it is used for area navigation (RNAV) systems as well as integrated systems containing loran and GPS sensors.

1. SOLID STATE TRANSMITTER
2. SIMULTANEOUS READOUT OF DIST., GS, & TTS
3. INTERNAL OR REMOTE CHANNELING
4. COMPLETELY PANEL MOUNTED
5. OPERATES 11 - 33 VDC

Bendix/King KN64 panel-mounted DME.

INSTALLATION TIPS

Because of the operating frequency range of the DME, its antenna doesn't have the same ground plane requirement like those for ADF and VHF type equipment. As a precautionary measure, however, to prevent interference from noise generators, the transponder, other avionics, or possible intermittent loss of range due to P-static, it's strongly suggested that you specify the same installation and bonding techniques that would be used for any antenna installation.

DME is similar to transponders in that they are both pulse systems. The key difference is in the interrogation process. The DME interrogates the ground station and receives a return signal that provides the information used for the display. Transponders are interrogated by radar systems on the ground.

Because DME and transponders operate similarly and on frequencies that are close together but not the same, the two systems can interfere with each other. This problem is most prevalent when the two systems' antennas are closer than 3 feet together. If the two systems are interfering with each other, it might be necessary to install a suppression cable between the DME and transponder. The suppression system shuts the DME off for a very short period of time while the transponder is being interrogated to prevent the DME from interfering with transponder operation. With proper antenna placement, installation of the suppression system usually isn't necessary. Many avionics shops will install the suppression system but not hook it up unless testing later shows that the DME is interfering with transponder operation. This can save you lots of money by allowing the suppression system to be hooked up if necessary without ripping up the upholstery to install one if it has been left out. It isn't a good idea to hook up the suppression system if it's not needed because it can reduce the performance of the DME.

DME antennas are either the cheap, rod/ball type or the short, little fin-type blade. Transponders use the same antenna, and both types are installed on the belly of the airplane. The cheaper rod antenna performs fine but is much more susceptible to damage, especially by ham-fisted airplane washers or careless mechanics. The more expensive blade antenna is a better choice for both systems. It will withstand considerable stress, particularly the long arm of the airplane washer. The DME antenna should be installed preferably 6 feet from the transponder antenna and at least 3 feet from ADF and communications antennas.

The DME is highly sensitive to low-current availability, so be sure that the proper size wiring is used in the installation. Errors caused by improper wiring could cause only a small change in distance but will have a greater effect on speed readout.

If you're replacing an old DME with a new one, consider redoing the entire installation. The older the wiring, the higher the probability it's been damaged or weakened by nicks, chafing, or cracking of insulation. Because the old switches and circuit breakers have seen a lot of use, it's also highly possible that their demise is close at hand. Better to be safe and replace those worn items while the airplane is all torn apart than to have to tear it apart again sometime in the future when a knotty problem shows up.

DME PROBLEMS

Important note: due to the high power output of the DME, damage to the DME's receiver/transmitter can occur if you turn the unit on with the antenna coaxial cable disconnected. Although some units are designed to transmit with the antenna disconnected, most are not. To avoid an expensive trip to the shop, don't run the DME with its antenna disconnected.

When experiencing intermittent DME operation, you can check if the antenna is causing a problem if you can tune in a DME station from where you're located on the ground. With the DME tuned in, try *gently* tapping the DME antenna with a long wood dowel or broom handle. Do not touch the antenna while the system is on. If the rod-type antenna has been bent or broken, the distance readout will drop off and start again while you tap the antenna. Believe it or not, I've seen cases where someone, an airplane washer or mechanic, broke the rod-type antenna and simply stuffed the rod back into the antenna base, hoping no one would notice it had been broken. Sometimes these broken antennas would work for a while, but they always had to be replaced.

The tougher blade antennas can cause problems. Some of the older Narco blade antennas delaminate internally, causing the metal element to vibrate until the fragile connection to the internal connector is broken.

When experiencing DME problems, first try tuning another station. DME stations can handle only a certain amount of interrogators, and if you are one too many, your DME won't be able to lock onto the station. Before spending too much time on troubleshooting a faulty DME, ask your avionics shop to perform a ramp test with their test set. If the system still shows no signs of life, go through the following tests.

If it's a groundspeed problem, remove the unit and have it bench checked.

If the DME doesn't function at all, you'll need to check that the system is getting proper power and is properly grounded, using a voltmeter.

When the DME breaks lock with a station or seems to be weak, note if you can receive the audio signal (Morse code ID every 30 seconds). Also, were you flying directly to or from the station? Accuracy is better during a direct, head-on approach. Remember that the DME computes slant range, so accuracy is quite good at a distance, but both distance and groundspeed information are affected by how close you are to the transmitter. When you approach the station, the groundspeed readout will slow, then rapidly increase as you fly over the station.

Reception of a strong audio signal from the station is a positive indication that the antenna system is intact and that the failure is most likely in the receiver/transmitter. This isn't always true, however, because a poorly bonded antenna can cause DME problems. For this reason, it is important that a DME antenna that is mounted on an access panel be well bonded to the panel and the panel bonded to the airframe.

One problem that occurs frequently is a squawk that the DME isn't working in the "remote" switch position because the pilot didn't have the nav 1/nav 2 switch set properly. While the problem could be in the wiring for that switch, the first thing to check is if you had the switch correctly set.

Sometimes the DME works fine with the engine running but not on battery power alone. If so, the DME's power supply is deteriorated or undersized wiring was installed. If the wiring was the wrong type, the DME may have worked fine initially when it was new, but as it gets older, the need for adequate supply current becomes greater. The longer the distance between components, the stronger the need for heavier-gauge wiring and coaxial cable. Don't scrimp on this during the installation.

DME MANUFACTURERS

The following DME manufacturers' addresses are listed in the Sources section at the end of this book.

Bendix/King

B.F. Goodrich Flight Systems

Collins Avionics

Narco Avionics

S-TEC

Sigma-Tek

13
Loran systems

NOW THAT THE SO-CALLED MID-CONTINENT GAP HAS BEEN CLOSED, THE only thing that's keeping pilots from installing loran (long-range navigation) has been the emergence of the amazing global positioning system (GPS). This might be premature. The FAA, at the time of this writing, is still working on loran IFR approach certification, and loran transmitter chains are still expanding throughout South and Central America, the Caribbean, Canada, and Commonwealth of Independent States (former Soviet Union). The continued financial investment in loran transmitter sites through much of the world suggests that we can expect to see loran around for years to come.

LORAN VERSUS GPS

GPS is here and the entire complement of satellites needed to make GPS reliable and accessible 24 hours a day should be in place by the time you read this or shortly thereafter. There are, however, FAA restrictions on how GPS interfaces with the airplane that severely limit its use as a navigational tool, especially if you want to hook it up to drive an autopilot. GPS is very accurate, but until the government decides to officially make the signals available to civilians, sudden shutdowns of the system can take place without warning. This happened recently, where some airplane owners visited their avionics shop for a GPS problem only to find that the system had been shut off temporarily.

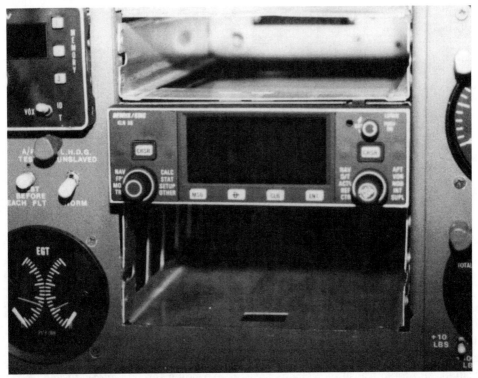

The installer must find room in an already crowded instrument panel for this Bendix/King KLN88 loran. The goal is to relocate equipment as necessary while retaining cosmetic and functional appeal.

For the time being, loran and GPS together form the nucleus of a reliable navigation system that could eventually prove to be more reliable than existing VHF VOR systems. Combining loran with GPS was originally a marriage of convenience, but it will be necessary for the near future. Loran is not as accurate as GPS, but it is certified for IFR enroute and IFR approaches (although published loran approaches are few and far between). GPS is currently undergoing approach testing and still isn't approved for enroute IFR.

One of the strengths of IFR-certified lorans is the ability to use it for new approaches that are expected to be published soon. Short of making an approach using DME or an ILS, a properly certified loran can follow a preplanned flight plan right down to the centerline of the destination airport with a high degree of accuracy. This alternative to conventional approaches is particularly advantageous for airports that lack ILS equipment. While there aren't many approved loran approaches yet, there should be more in the pipeline. It could be years before we see GPS approaches because to provide GPS approach capability, additional ground-to-satellite interface equipment will need to be installed.

At the time this was written, the FAA announced that GPS can be used for VFR navigation only, not for IFR navigation. Just two years ago, the FAA released a letter in which it stated that "standalone GPS equipment cannot be approved for navigation at this time," so the situation is progressing, albeit slowly. Any limitations on the use of an installed GPS system will have to be listed in the flight manual and detailed in an instrument panel placard such as "GPS not to be used for IFR navigation."

Multi-sensor navigation units with built-in loran and GPS are becoming more popular. When one of the sensors fail, the unit must warn the pilot that they can no longer rely on the failed sensor. If the unit, say, is an IFR-approved loran and VFR-approved GPS and the loran sensor fails, then the unit must warn the pilot that the unit can no longer be used for IFR navigation. At present, then, GPS is providing backup for loran, while in the future, when GPS IFR approval occurs, loran will be the backup for the more accurate GPS.

Because loran started out as a nav system for boats, the transmitters are maintained by the U.S. Coast Guard, while the FAA monitors the accuracy and reliability of the network. Manufacturers of loran and GPS receivers have spent a lot of time designing easy-to-use nav systems at a reasonable price. You have the option of picking the unit that fits your navigation needs and budget, from a basic unit to one with all the bells and whistles.

HOW LORAN WORKS

Loran works by measuring differences in the time that two different signals are received from two different loran stations. Because loran signals are low frequency, the loran system is subject to errors that plague all low-frequency systems (like ADFs). These include day-night effects, shoreline effects, and weather effects. These sources of possible errors make it difficult to predict the reliable accuracy of loran signals, so for loran to be used for IFR approaches, the FAA has had to install signal monitors all over the U.S. to make sure signals are accurate while aircraft are flying approaches. This is the major reason why loran approaches have taken so long to be implemented. There are still very few actual approaches in use. More sophisticated loran receivers can obtain data from multiple transmitter chains, hence the term *multichain receiver*.

Loran will be around for several more years, so waiting for GPS might not be the best policy if you need sophisticated navigation capability now. You might want to consider buying a nav management system like Narco's Star*Nav or II Morrow's Model 2001 and attaching the sensors you desire as they become available or you can afford them. Start with a loran sensor and work your way up to GPS.

Other considerations, which apply obviously to any radio, are warranty and post-sale support. Also, with navigation systems, how much will database updates cost you? Make sure to evaluate the visibility of the unit's display before you make your purchase decision. LCD displays, for example, can be very difficult to read in direct sunlight. You don't want to find out that you can't live with the display after you've spent a couple thousand dollars.

LORAN RECEIVERS

Following are descriptions of various units offered by nav system manufacturers. Rather than suggest which unit is best, the information is presented on each manufacturer's product so that you can make an educated decision as to what will suit your needs. A discussion of installation tips follows these descriptions, including ideas for loran antenna installations because these tend to be very sensitive to poor installation practices.

Arnav systems

Arnav has managed to keeps its customers happy by maintaining the old R-50 layout and exterior appearance while bringing the new R-50i into the 21st century with multichain capability and a host of other new features. The R50 continues as Arnav's VFR loran offering, and the R50i is now the FMS 5000, which is IFR certifiable and available with an optional GPS sensor.

The FMS 5000 is a close competitor to the Bendix/King KLN88 and Trimble and Northstar lorans with its IFR certifiable capability. Its predecessor, the R-50, is a good unit, but lacks the multichain tracking technology. A Jeppesen NavData database card plugs into the front of the FMS 5000, making it very easy to update. The receiver will track up to 12 stations simultaneously, automatically selecting the most accurate signals. An exact digital display of distance off course and direction to fly to the course is provided to the pilot. When pulling up the name of a waypoint, it isn't necessary to enter the whole name of the waypoint. Just enter the initial character and the rest of the name is filled in automatically on the 40-character LED display.

Coupled with a GPS sensor, the FMS 5000 delivers respectable performance. Each sensor is used to calculate the aircraft's position, and the best of the two positions is displayed on the LED display. With the ability to deliver accurate performance up to speeds of Mach 2, the FMS 5000 is suitable for corporate and commercial jets. The unit is IFR certifiable under FAA Advisory Circular AC20-121A and it is approved for primary enroute and terminal navigation under TSO C60b. The FMS 5000 also incorporates air data computer interfaces.

FMS 5000 nav management features include: minimum safe altitudes, vertical nav (VNAV), true airspeed, winds aloft, fuel calculations, and digital track guidance indicator and CDI settings of one quarter and one mile. Like the Northstar, the antenna has a preamplifier so you must use the supplied antenna. An RS-232 port allows the FMS 5000 to be interfaced with fuel computers for enroute fuel consumption and planning purposes plus the unit can be hooked up to the Artex Aircraft Supplies ELS-10 emergency locator transmitter. If your airplane is equipped with an FMS 5000 hooked up to an ELS-10 and you have an accident that activates the ELT, the ELS-10 will not only broadcast the standard ELT signal but your latitude and longitude as well. (Arnav sold its ELT business to Artex.)

To make it more user friendly, every FMS 5000 comes with a portable power supply for at-home flight planning and practice. It is obvious that, under new management, Arnav is designing their unit to be a true flight management system, making it more adaptable to the wave of technological changes sweeping the aviation community.

Bendix/King

Bendix/King waited in the wings for some time, absorbing the advantages of competitive units before revealing the graphical display, IFR-certified KLN88 loran. The company's time was evidently well spent, for the unit was highly praised by the press and passed muster with those customers who were lucky enough to be the first to test the new unit.

If all but the basic features are ignored, the KLN88 is very user friendly. The inner knobs operate like chapters in a book, while the outer, smaller knobs are used to turn the pages. As pages are "turned," the "page number" is displayed on the CRT screen. A direct and obvious approach to setting up the controls is the fact that the left knobs operate the left side of the display and the right knobs operate the right-hand side. "Direct-to" navigation is as simple as pushing a button, selecting the identifier for the destination, then depressing "enter" to view data. Press "enter" once again and the waypoint is activated. For those already familiar with loran, it won't take long to get up and running with the KLN88. If you're just getting started, read the manual.

One key feature that has had both a positive and negative impact on customers is the large 3.3-inch (diagonal) TV-tube display, which can provide a wealth of data for a careful user. Those who don't take time to read the well-written and highly descriptive manual will have some difficulty with the loran and probably won't use all of its operational capabilities. It takes about three hours to read the manual and an hour of hands-on practice with the KLN88 to become competent to the point where you can make use of all the features and plan your first IFR flight. It's not difficult, it just takes time. Taking that time can reap great benefits, especially if you're approaching a strange new airport. One of the greatest strengths of the KLN88 is its ability to show you the way across the country, then blend the flight plan, almost imperceptibly, into the approach.

Most pilots who use the KLN88 enjoy the unique ability of being able to see a graphical display of changing courses, waypoints, even identifiers and other navigational information with the turn of a knob. No scrolling is necessary, all selected data is portrayed on the big screen at one time. You can even program personal data about, say, which FBO rents cars or your favorite airport restaurants.

Another unique option is the ability of the display to provide, on a split screen, both a CDI on one side and the graphic map on the other. Most pilots will elect to set the screen to full map display as it will provide all the data needed for a long flight. Flight planning is easy, although taking the unit home is better on your airplane's batteries and gives you plenty of time to set up your flights with your charts spread out on the living room floor. Of course you can make changes while airborne, but minor changes are easier while flying than trying to enter entire batches of data while turbulence is bouncing you around.

By any standard, the KLN88 is a good choice. Besides being able to provide one or more graphic maps, CDI, waypoints, altitude prompts, trip planning, fuel management, flight service frequencies, and a bunch of other goodies, the screen can also be used to solve true airspeed, pressure altitude, density, altitude, winds aloft, and temperature and speed conversion problems.

The database contains over 40,000 elements, all public-use runways (1000 feet or longer), all VORs, NDBs, airway intersections, outer markers, 250 user-defined waypoints, airspace boundaries, and more. The database can also handle flights to Central America, the Caribbean, and Canada.

There is no preamplifier on the KLN88 antenna, just a coaxial cable from the antenna to the receiver, so you aren't restricted to one type of antenna and can use any decent loran antenna. There are three antenna types available: a high-speed blade antenna, a straight rod, and a bent rod. There are times when the bent rod will be subject to noise problems, although it's rare.

B.F. Goodrich Flight Systems (formerly Foster AirData systems)

As the trend goes with the rest of the avionics industry, so goes B.F. Goodrich Flight Systems. The company created the LNS6000, a flight management system that can accept four or more sensor inputs to provide the most accurate possible positional fix. GPS and loran is provided internally, while DME, TACAN, and VLF/Omega signals can be blended from external sources to provide not only national, but global navigation guidance. The premise is similar to the computerized method employed by other manufacturers. Each sensor input is weighed against each other and against known positions within the database to arrive at a positional fix that is more accurate than any of the individual sensor fixes.

The database contains over 40,000 data points with expandability to over 150,000 for future growth. Every 28 days, upgrades are available and can be input by users with a credit card-size data card. Over 100 three-dimensional flight plans with up to 99 waypoints per flight plan can be entered and called up by airport identifiers, by city and state, or by airport name. Although flight plans can be entered and locked, they can be updated and modified enroute. After the flight, the modified "locked" flight plans will revert to their original configuration.

In May 1991, B.F. Goodrich Flight Systems purchased the Stormscope line from 3M, and the company plans interfacing options with the Stormscope and even with TCAS (traffic collision and avoidance system). Flight Systems advertises that regardless of the changes in avionics, the LNS6000 will be ready. Imagine flying along a preplanned route and suddenly the LNS6000 receives data from the Stormscope warning of impending severe weather ahead. The pilot can make immediate changes in course to avoid the turbulent and dangerous conditions, and once past it, returns back to the original planned course without confusing or elaborate modification of the flight plan. The same will be true when interfaced with TCAS; after an avoidance maneuver, the flight will be back on track, thanks to the LNS6000.

What is so unusual about the LNS6000 as opposed to other manufacturers' systems is its shape and size. Unlike most lorans, which require a conventional 6.25-inch by 2-inch hole, the LNS6000 fits a 3-inch-square panel cutout (a standard Arinc 3ATI-size hole). The unit is professional looking and provides a sophisticated nav management system in a small amount of panel space. The square shape can be especially advantageous with today's crowded panels.

B.F. Goodrich Flight Systems also offers the Foster LNS616B, IFR certified for enroute and approach modes. Both loran and DME form the sensor heart of this reliable, long-range navigation system.

B.F. Goodrich Flight Systems hasn't forgotten light aircraft owners and offers some cost-effective and highly accurate lorans. The F14, a standard panel-mount configuration, offers IFR certifiability, easy programming, and an LED display. This also comes with a take-home power supply for practice and flight planning. At the bottom of the list is the Foster 500, not IFR certifiable, but still a competent loran that offers a database cartridge update, user friendly interface, and highly accurate point-to-point navigation.

II Morrow

II Morrow is dedicated to providing a selection of lorans that meet the needs of a variety of customers. There are six different models, from one end of the financial and technological spectrum to the other.

The Flybuddy loran is at the low end of the spectrum for several reasons. It isn't IFR certifiable, uses a less expensive LCD display, and does not conform to TSO requirements. Don't let that sway you, however: the Flybuddy is packed with features that read like a Who's Who of lorans. The Flybuddy has been very popular with the single-engine crowd. It includes an RS-232 port for interfacing with fuel management systems, moving maps, and properly equipped ELTs. It has a database with airport information, navaids, and more, and is updated using a replaceable data card.

The star of II Morrow's line is the Apollo Navigation Management System (NMS). This isn't a loran or GPS by itself, but it manages the sensor input of several external systems and displays the output on its bright, easy-to-read LED screen. As many as two lorans and two GPS sensors can be interfaced with the NMS. Another alternative could include one loran sensor, one fuel flow and air data connection, or an additional display for the copilot. It sounds confusing, but the main thing to remember is that this unit allows considerable variation in inputs. The Apollo NMS can feed moving maps, fuel flow indicators, altitude encoders, CDIs, HSIs, and provide vertical deviation information, making it a very comprehensive system for the money. Up to 255 sensor inputs can be supported by the Apollo NMS, allowing constant adaptability to present and future navigation technology.

Over 31 custom fields of data can be displayed on the Apollo NMS's NMC 2001 three-line LED screen by selecting custom pages, which are limited only by the number of modules connected. The unit's loran sensor is designed to track up to 12 stations simultaneously, automatically selecting the best of all available chains for the most accurate position. Optional selection of up to four antennas is available, too. The GPS portion is a five-channel, fast-sequencing system with a remote-mounted sensor. The optional fuel flow sensor requires interfacing with static, pitot, OAT, and XYZ output from an HSI or RMI.

The panel-mounted NMC (nav management computer) of the Apollo NMS is available as either a standard panel-mount unit (the NMC 2001) or as a Dzus rail-mount configuration (NMC 2001D).

Narco

For those who already have a loran and would like to add GPS, the autoscanning, multisensor Star*Nav by Narco is just the ticket. The Star*Nav multisensor navigational computer contains a loran sensor and offers much more than stand-alone loran boxes.

Star*Nav comes with a Jeppesen NavData database card that inserts into the front of the unit. The Star*Nav isn't IFR certified yet, but should be soon. Star*Nav is actually a 20-channel VOR receiver with 40-channel glideslope, DME, and loran sensor that blends signals from a variety of sources, referenced against the database, to provide the most accurate navigation information to the pilot. The Star*Nav NS-9000 can be used as a basic VOR/glideslope nav unit, but its real beauty shines though when it also can access loran and DME information to help you get where you're going.

After being initialized, the Star*Nav, with its two integral computers, will search the internal database, looking for the nearest 10 VOR and DME stations. The system will reference, through triangulation, signal strength and distance from several VOR and DME stations that give the most accurate information out of the 10 stations it is searching. The unit selects the two VOR and DME stations that can provide the best accuracy and uses that data to compute four latitude and longitude fixes and distance information. The loran information is blended with the VOR/DME data to provide even more accurate navigational data. DME slant range distance is corrected for altitude to provide even better accuracy. The computer calculates the most accurate position possible given the inputs it has to deal with and discards all other readings. If one of the sensor inputs should become too weak to be useful, or fail altogether, its input is discarded and the remaining sensors are used to provide accurate navigation data.

Flying direct has never been easier. Not only does the Star*Nav satisfy FAA requirements for enroute IFR, but it is also approved for approaches because primary navigation is predicated on the VOR information, loran being used only as reference data.

A lower-cost NS-925 version is available that has only the VOR and glideslope receivers built in, but not the loran, GPS, or DME. The NS-925 can be hooked up to external loran, GPS, and DME units, however, for effective multisensor navigation.

Northstar

Born of a company that made the word "loran" synonymous with reliability, Northstar manufacturer Digital Marine Electronics Corp. won the National Marine Electronics Associate award for best loran in performance and reliability for virtually every year the award was given. The company's Northstar Avionics division was formed to produce and market the Northstar M1, developed specifically for the aviation market to fulfill demand for an easy-to-use accurate aviation loran. Although not IFR certifiable, the original M1 has proven to be highly precise and reliable, even in areas where other lorans' performance declines. Northstar recently sold its general aviation loran and GPS receiver products to Canadian Marconi, but this hasn't slowed development and marketing of Northstar's aviation products.

With all the competitors releasing IFR-certified lorans, it was no surprise that Northstar entered that market as well, but it did so by designing a new unit, the M2, available with both loran and GPS sensors or loran alone. The M2 is as easy to use as the original M1. In fact, it's hard to tell the difference at first glance. The main difference is the M1's database is built-in and thus upgradeable by the factory, where the M2's database can be updated by the user with an update card. There is nothing complicated or gimmicky about the M1 and M2, but you should read the manual just like with any new piece of equipment. Unlike most other lorans, the display on the Northstar is easy to see, even in direct sunlight where other companies' offerings fall flat.

A built-in CDI helps you navigate direct to any waypoint. Dual readouts show distance and bearing on one readout with course, speed, ETE, or another waypoint on the other. By entering compass heading and true airspeed, winds aloft will be displayed. A database with over 20,000 waypoints, 7,400 airports, 1,200 VORs, 2,000 NDBs, 10,000 intersections, and 250 user-programmable waypoints is available at the turn of a knob.

Unlike the Bendix/King KLN88, the M1 and M2 have a preamplifier located in the antenna, which precludes the use of a third-party antenna. Location of this antenna and coaxial cable routing is critical. P-static, onboard noise generators, and other related noise contaminates can severely degrade the quality of the received signal and prevent the receiver from functioning properly (see antenna installation tips later in this chapter).

Northstar M1 owners can upgrade to GPS, too, without buying a new receiver. Northstar offers the M2V field upgrade kit, which incorporates the Model 8100A six-channel GPS sensor and turns the M1 into a full loran/GPS receiver.

Terra

Terra's loran is a good, basic unit, not IFR certifiable, but it works quite well for a low-end loran. There is no database, so more work is required from the pilot to enter waypoints. An LED light on the face of the unit will blink should the internal battery need replacing or if the received signal is too weak for navigation. The display is a planar gas discharge type with 32 characters.

The terra loran features 120 user-enterable waypoints, either latitude/longitude or bearing and distance from another waypoint. Waypoints are stored in alphabetical order. Up to four flight plans with nine waypoints each can be stored. The internal lithium battery will maintain waypoints data for up to five years. Time to track is two minutes, and the unit will track at speeds up to 500 knots. A built-in preamplifier is provided with the whip antenna that comes with the loran. If you wish to use a long-wire antenna, the preamplifier is remote.

Texas instruments

Sorry, but TI doesn't make lorans anymore. However, the company will update your TI loran to allow navigation in the mid-continent gap if you haven't had it updated yet. For the update, send your TI loran to: Texas Instruments, 6600 Chase Oak Blvd., M.S. 8462, Building SK3, Plano, TX 75023. The phone number is (800) 336-5236, extension 9400. Some former TI dealers can do the upgrade as well. The cost for TI to do the upgrade is $395 plus tax and shipping.

Trimble

Trimble's unit was originally released as a GPS system, but the company realized that its unit would better fit the general aviation market if accompanied with a loran sensor to provide IFR certification and redundancy. Trimble's all-digital Model 3000 is that unit, a combined loran and six-channel GPS with advanced multichain tracking and excellent noise-rejection capability. This user-friendly unit allows pilots to use the loran part of the unit just as they did the GPS unit, so there is no learning curve when switching to the Model 3000.

The Model 3000 includes a complete Jeppesen worldwide database (NavData card) of global aviation information that includes VORs, NDBs, airway intersections, airspace boundaries, MEAs, and airports throughout the world, including those in Russian and former Soviet bloc (CIS) countries. When all features are active, the Model 3000 functions as a flight management system, allowing immediate access to all the data provided in the database. Two lines of 20-character, high-intensity, orange alphanumeric LEDs allow you to display groundspeed, time enroute, course deviation, and much more.

One feature that has gained support from the turboprop and jet crowd is Trimble's Model 3100. Quick-release Dzus fasteners make it easy to remove the 3100 for maintenance or updating. Presumably these types of airplanes are usually kept in secure hangars, so theft of easy-to-remove avionics is probably not that big a problem.

ANTENNA INSTALLATION

Antennas are the sensors of avionics systems, a possible weak link if not given the attention they deserve. Their location and mounting method should be such that no matter how the aircraft is maneuvered, there will be no alteration in the received signal and resultant reduction in quality of the equipment's displayed information.

Four types of antennae are available:

- For helicopters and low-speed aircraft, use a low-profile bent-blade or bent-whip antenna.
- For top mounting in light aircraft, use a heavy stick type or blade antenna.
- Use a blade-type antenna for pressurized, high speed aircraft.
- Long-wire antennas require the use of a preamplifier and are no longer used for modern loran installations.

The antenna can be mounted on the top or bottom of the fuselage. Make sure a doubler or backing plate is used to maintain the structural integrity of the skin where the antenna is installed and that all mating surfaces are corrosion-proofed and properly bonded.

Loran antennas must be located at least 24 inches from VHF and HF antennas and 4 feet from DME or transponder antennas to prevent interference. If your installation requires an antenna preamplifier, the distance between the preamp and other antennas should be a minimum of 3 feet. If you can't install the antenna per the loran manufacturer's recommendations and you're forced to locate it near noise generators or other obstructions, then skin mapping might be necessary. This involves testing the loran while hooked up to an antenna that you can move around to find the best location on the airframe. Once you find the best location, the antenna can be installed permanently.

Some other constraints that dictate loran antenna location are as follows:

- Avoid areas of electrical noise such as strobes, rotating beacons, electrical actuators.
- You need physically unobstructed reception.
- You need good bonding to airframe.
- Antenna needs a good ground plane (18 to 24 square inches of unobstructed metal around the antenna).
- Avoid locating antenna near windshields and nonconductive panels that could build up static charges.

The best location for the loran antenna is high on the upper fuselage, but also acceptable is the lower aft fuselage on the swept-up portion of the tailcone. Although noise levels are normally lower on the bottom of the tailcone, obstructions can be more prevalent, causing possible blanking of the received signal. One thing that might help for a tailcone antenna is bonding the forward nose gear doors on two or three hinge points. Static charges that build up on unbonded doors can act as a barrier, effectively preventing signals from arriving at the antenna.

If mounting the antenna on a contoured surface, you might have to create a flat, conductive surface on which to mount the antenna or install spacers to allow the base of the antenna to bond thoroughly to the airframe.

Because lorans are particularly sensitive to P-static, treat the antenna with kid gloves. To minimize P-static effects, mount the antenna according to the manufacturer's recommendations. Most loran antennas are already prepared with anti-static coatings, but if in doubt, ask the installers to apply an additional coat.

Make sure the entire airframe is properly bonded, not just the loran installation itself. An ohmic survey of the airframe's bonding should show bonding resistance less than 3 mΩ.

LORAN INSTALLATION TIPS

Originally a marine nav aid, loran was designed to work best using the consistent conductivity of the salty ocean, but now that loran is used over land also, it has inherent problems not associated with marine use. With a low-frequency signal, loran is affected by the same atmospheric and electric storm phenomena like thunderstorms, P-static, sleet, and rain that cause ADF problems. We can't ignore these problems when installing a loran system.

P-static is a cancer that attacks the incoming signal, shakes it up and shuffles it around until the receiver hears only noise and shuts down. You can avoid P-static problems with a proper installation. Here are some ideas to help prevent this annoying and sometimes difficult to eliminate problem:

- If not already installed, add static discharge wicks to trailing edges of wings and control surfaces to discharge electrical charges harmlessly into the atmosphere. Replace static wicks periodically to ensure they can do their job efficiently. I don't recommend the carbon-wick type because of its high wear rate. Use the high-resistance rod and metal-pin-style wicks.
- Use good RF bonding procedures for all equipment. This includes bonding straps, removal of corrosion between components, and application of corrosion-proofing solutions like Alodine to bare-metal mating surfaces.
- Use antennas that have P-static resistant coatings, or spray antennas with anti-static coatings.
- Torque all antenna fasteners to equal values appropriate to fastener size.
- If using a wire-type antenna, the wire's insulation must be intact from one end of the wire to the other.
- If the skin or antenna attachment point isn't metal, install a ground plane.
- Keep antennas as far as possible from all nonconductive surfaces such as windshields and composite skins that aren't treated with conductive coatings. Com-

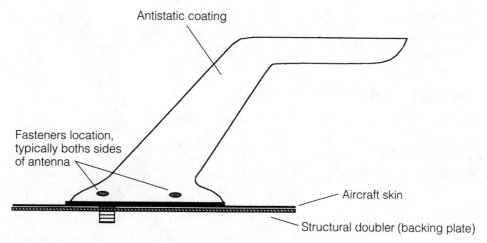

Loran blade antenna, suitable for high-speed aircraft.

posite skins can be treated with a conductive coating that will conduct static charges onto metal surfaces and out to static wicks.

• Mount antennas at least 24 to 36 inches from obstructions such as other antennas or airframe surfaces like stabilizers, landing gear legs, etc.

Avoid routing wiring in parallel or close proximity to wiring for pulse equipment like DME and transponders. To reduce potential induction of unwanted noise, cross these wires at 90-degree angles to each other.

The loran should be connected into your existing cooling-air setup for your installation. If you don't already have a cooling fan installed and a plenum (chamber that directs cooling air) mounted to the radio rack, see if you can't have it done as part of the loran installation. All modern radios must have a cooling fan for reliable operation at high cockpit temperatures. (See chapter 4.)

LORAN MANUFACTURERS

The following loran manufacturers are listed in the Sources section at the end of this book.

Arnav Systems

Bendix/King

B.F. Goodrich Flight Systems

II Morrow

Narco Avionics

Northstar Avionics
Terra Avionics
Trimble Navigation

LORAN CDI MANUFACTURERS

See Sources for addresses of these loran CDI manufacturers.

BVR Aero Precision
Mid-Continent Instrument

14
Global positioning system

THE GLOBAL POSITIONING SYSTEM (GPS) IS THE MOST EXCITING AND accurate navigation system yet devised. The U.S. military created the global positioning system in 1973, but because the FAA wasn't involved in the creation of this sophisticated navigation system, the transition to permitting civilian use of GPS has been slow.

Luckily, no one has tried to charge a fee to pilots to use GPS thus far, even though it is tremendously expensive. Not only is there tremendous cost in building the system's satellites, but the satellites' launch and ongoing maintenance is incredibly expensive. Some estimate GPS costs more than $1 billion per year versus the $60 million per year spent on ground-based navigation systems. The planned 7.5-year lifespan of each GPS satellite is conservative and the satellites should nearly double that lifespan with an operational capability of 10 to 13 years.

GPS became part of the World Radio Navigation plans in late 1983 after the U.S. offered the system for civilian use. The first satellite was launched in 1978, and at the time, no one could predict whether the military would permit civilian use of GPS. The future of GPS looks bright, but could depend on consumer demand and potential political roadblocks.

The Garmin GPS 100 is easy to install, and the price is reasonable.

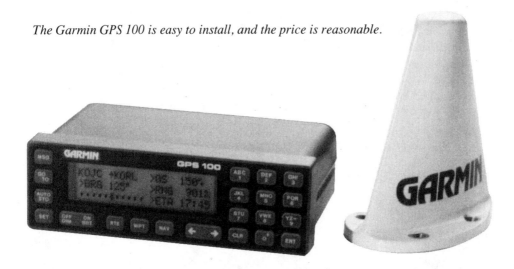

GPS is funded by the military, as is the Russian counterpart GLONASS. The two systems aren't compatible, but they could be interfaced given some modifications to our receivers and mutual cooperation between our nations. It won't be big news if this never happens, our system is expensive enough without having to spend more to interface it with the Russian system, which is much more expensive due to shorter satellite lifespan.

Before GPS, the most accurate system we had was DME. While both systems are time-based and can display accurate distance and time-to-station information, GPS can do much more. It is far more accurate and can provide this accuracy in terms of position anywhere on the surface of the earth and also vertical position. In other words, GPS can report your altitude over the earth with pinpoint precision, making GPS a truly three-dimensional navigation system.

GPS is composed of 24 satellites in six orbital planes, with four satellites in each plane. As of this writing, there are 21 satellites now in orbit. Three of the 24 satellites will be in-orbit spares to provide backup should any of the primary satellites fail. The satellites orbit the earth every 12 hours at 10,898 nautical miles above the surface. From any point on earth at any time, vehicles with GPS receivers will have from six to ten satellites in "view." Standard positioning service signals are broadcast on a single frequency in the L-band of the radio frequency spectrum. To assure accuracy, atomic clocks accurate to within one second every 70,000 years are part of the satellites' timing circuits.

The U.S. Air Force's Second Satellite Control Squadron at Colorado Springs, Colorado, assigned to the Second Space Wing at Falcon Air Force Station, is responsible for monitoring and controlling GPS. This unit is responsible for receiving information from five other monitoring stations, evaluating the data, making corrections, and up-linking that information to the satellites three times a day. The other five monitoring stations are at Onizuka AFS in Hawaii, Cape Canaveral in Florida, Ascension in the South Atlantic, Diego Garcia in the Indian Ocean, and Kwajalein in the Central Pacific.

The advent of GPS could virtually eliminate the need for complex ground-based navigation systems and even relegate FAA's current radar setup to backup status. GPS could provide primary position and altitude data to FAA center controllers quicker and more accurately than the current radar system, but any such transition is way in the future. Even with growing use of GPS, the current VOR/DME system is going to be around for a long time.

The GPS Team won 1992 Collier Trophy for "the most significant development for safe and efficient navigation . . . since the introduction of radio navigation 50 years ago." The GPS development team includes: U.S. Air Force, U.S. Naval Research Laboratory, The Aerospace Corp., Rockwell International, and IBM Federal Systems. The trophy was awarded by the National Aeronautic Association.

An indication of how popular GPS receivers are becoming is that during 1992, GPS receivers outsold loran receivers 13,110 to 5,600 according to the Aircraft Electronics Association. In 1991, the numbers were reversed with 3,300 GPS receivers sold and 8,000 loran. The GPS number includes hand-held GPS receivers and combined loran/GPS receivers.

HOW GPS WORKS

Although the technology behind GPS is highly complex, the basic theory isn't. The satellites are reference points, and position is calculated from distance measurements to the satellites. Four satellites are required for accurate position determination, but as few as three will work in most cases, with high velocity and certain locations being the exception. Receivers that can receive and process eight or more satellites at one time are the most accurate because the receiver can determine which geometry (which signals of those received from the eight satellites) is the most accurate. Even if all satellites aren't visible to the receiver, altitude sensors tied into the GPS receiver could replace some of the satellite data, reducing dependency on at least one satellite.

With distance measurement accomplished via signal timing, the clocks on the satellites and in the receiver must be highly accurate. Quartz-clock technology made it possible to manufacture a receiver with reasonably accurate measuring capability, up to 0.000000001 second accuracy. Although accurate by most standards, the receiver clock isn't precise enough, but trigonometry calculations cancel any inaccuracies that occur.

The basic premise behind GPS is the time measurement it takes for a satellite signal to arrive at the receiver. To do this, the satellite generates a pseudo-random code and simultaneously the air-, ground-, or water-based receiver generates its own pseudo-random code. When the receiver finds a match for the satellite's random code, then the receiver calculates the time difference between the two codes, which, along with calculations from time differences generated by at least two more satellites, displays location and other calculated information such as speed, time to destination, etc.

Your receiver must receive signals from at least three satellites for an accurate position to be displayed.

Knowing a little about signal processing will help you decide which GPS to purchase. GPS receivers are advertised as one-, two-, four-, or more channel systems. Many low-budget systems process only one satellite at a time. How fast the data is processed is also a factor of the receiver's capability. During the time processing is taking place, navigation is not occurring, and this can be up to 12.5 minutes for the slowest of receivers. For aircraft, this would not be acceptable, but for a slow-moving boat, maybe. We can expect these capabilities to change as manufacturing technology becomes more sophisticated. Someday building a GPS receiver will be as commonplace as manufacturing a CD or stereo player for your car.

Engineers are designing faster-sequencing receivers that track as many satellites as needed. The drawback is the signal-to-noise ratios (SNR). On a single-channel receiver, SNR is reduced by a factor of four during the time sequencing (switching between satellites) takes place. Designing a single-channel receiver is much cheaper, and it's easier to keep SNR down to reasonable levels. With a two-channel receiver, SNR is reduced by a factor of two, and the more channels, the higher the potential SNR and the more work goes into trying to "design out" the harmful, high SNR.

An analogy of SNR might be like comparing water flow from the faucet with the amount of contamination it contains. The greater the ratio of water, the healthier it is. The greater the ratio of contamination, the less healthy the water. With avionics, the greater the amount of noise received, the less the amount of quality signal that can be received and processed reliably. This is a simplified explanation, but it should help begin to explain why receivers are so expensive to design and build.

A few detractors suggest that the four-channel units have a down side. While the aircraft is moving rapidly through the air, measurement of velocity is hampered by the unit cycling through the four channels. For the best of both worlds, they are recommending the two-channel units. These units process the data from the satellites in "leapfrog" fashion. While one channel is processing the information from one satellite, the next channel is busy acquiring its lock onto the next satellite. With this little electronic trick, no condition-fail message will occur, allowing continuous navigation.

If considering a GPS, don't be dissuaded by those who put it down. The FAA, as of this writing, just announced that GPS is now okayed for VFR navigation, and it still can be used as a backup for IFR and as reference data for certified sensors like loran and VOR/DME in some of the newer flight management systems. FAA's TSO C129 is the most recent standard for standalone GPS receivers. This will permit GPS to be used for IFR navigation, but only after the full complement of satellites is up and military and FAA plans for GPS use are finalized.

The civilian signals are purposely degraded by the U.S. military to an accuracy of slightly over 325 feet horizontally and 500 feet vertically, so the situation for GPS approaches is still uncertain, although testing is being done at this time. For point-to-point navigation, however, GPS is amazingly accurate. An example of the types of flights that GPS's accuracy makes possible is the global circumnavigation made by

Tom and Fran Towle in June 1990, as reported by *Aviation Consumer* magazine. The Towles flew from Miami to California, to Hawaii, then to the isolated, hard-to-find Christmas Island in the middle of the Pacific Ocean. The GPS came in very handy on the 2,446-mile stretch from Cape Verde to Barbados, West Indies. Sixty one days after they left, they returned to Miami, having logged 150 hours in their Cessna 310, ably assisted by twin panel-mounted Trimble GPS receivers.

GPS IFR APPROACHES

The FAA conducted testing of GPS IFR approaches using AOPA's Beech A36 beginning in late 1992. Assuming that GPS IFR approaches become reality at some point (perhaps even shortly after this book is published), initial approach certification will be at the more than 5000 airports with existing nonprecision approaches. Until new TSO standards are developed for GPS receivers to be used for IFR approaches, GPS nonprecision approaches will have to be flown using VOR/DME receivers or flight management systems as a backup.

GPS RECEIVERS

Which GPS unit should you select? The list of available receivers is growing, with prices dropping and features increasing. Manufacturers will continue to proliferate as more and more confidence in GPS is realized, by both the FAA and the flying public. Here are the most popular GPS receivers.

Arnav Systems

Arnav has entered the GPS market with a five-, six-, or twelve-channel GPS sensor that will interface with the company's FMS 5000 loran (formerly the R50i). Database updating is via the Jeppesen NavData card, without having to remove the receiver from the panel.

Arnav offers an extraordinary lifetime warranty for this unit, provided you install it per Arnav's recommendations with an avionics cooling fan and the proper tubing to direct cooling air onto the receiver.

Some of the features Arnav has introduced with the FMS 5000 loran GPS include automatic display of either loran or GPS information, depending on the best signal received, altitude display, vertical speed, annunciation of which nav sensor is being used, and pilot override, if necessary. The system will "cold start" or compute three-dimensional position within 6 minutes. Arnav also offers a GPS-only receiver, the Star 5000 five-channel GPS.

Bendix/King

Taking a page from the design of its successful KLN88 loran, Bendix/King now offers the similarly configured KLN90 GPS. The KLN90 can track up to eight satellites at a time and displays moving map navigation information on a crisp 3.3-inch diagonal CRT screen.

In addition to the choice of North American or worldwide Jeppesen NavData database, the KLN90 can store up to 250 user-defined waypoints and 26 programmable flight plans with up to 20 waypoints per flight plan. KLN90 owners can update the preprogrammed database using their own laptop computer, or for just the North American database, updates can be done via a cartridge on the back of the unit.

Other useful features of the KLN90 include VNAV advisories, instant display of air route traffic control center and flight service station frequencies based on your position, fuel management when interfaced with Shadin, Arnav, or Sheltech fuel management systems, air data display when interfaced with air data systems, flight calculations of such things as actual winds aloft, true airspeed, and density altitude, airspace alert for special-use airspace, and even display of runway diagrams for certain airports.

The KLN90 can provide location information for Artex's ELS-10 position-broadcasting ELT. Another important feature is the altitude alert function that notifies the pilot 1000 feet before reaching a preset target altitude, eliminating the need to install a separate altitude alert device and saving panel space.

An optional take-home case is offered, allowing the KLN90 owner to practice using the sophisticated GPS receiver at home or to perform flight-planning functions without draining the aircraft's battery.

Garmin

Garmin (previously known as Pronav) manufactures the GPS 100 and the GPS 100 AVD, both surprisingly inexpensive yet professional looking. The units feature a single-channel receiver that updates every second and will handle up to eight satellites at one time. An LCD screen and the single-channel receiver permits lower manufacturing costs while retaining accuracy and update speed of incoming satellite information. Garmin won't reveal exactly how it accomplishes this; the specifications are proprietary.

Selling for less than $3600, the GPS 100 AVD is supplied with a well-engineered, quality-built aircraft-specific rack that comes complete with coaxial cable. Using two entry holes through the faceplate of the receiver, you can release the receiver from the rack quite easily with two large pins supplied with the unit. Two spring-loaded release-assist devices sit in the back of the rack to both help you remove the unit and to keep tension against the spring-loaded retaining clips located on both sides of the rack. This is similar to Narco's release method, but with more design consideration for easy installation. The rack is very rugged, and besides being structurally well built, it also provides for easy hookup of left/right, warning, and moving-map interfaces.

Garmin's antenna is similar to the blade antenna used for DME or transponders. It is designed to both improve reception over the horizon and eliminate standing water problems. The company supplies plenty of high-quality coaxial cable along with the installation manual and pilot's operating guide. While the avionics are on, or the electrical system (depending on how you have it hooked up), the receiver's internal nicad battery recharges, so the GPS is always ready to continue providing navigation guidance should the aircraft's alternator fail and the main battery die. Don't forget to shut the GPS off when the airplane isn't running, however; otherwise, the internal battery won't be fully charged. You can, if you wish, remove the internal battery, in which case the Garmin acts like any other piece of avionics equipment, shutting off when you turn off the avionics master.

To prevent loss of input waypoints, another internal battery maintains waypoint memory for up to seven years.

There are four operational modes for this receiver. The first is normal mode, and the second is battery-saver mode. The third mode, called Quick Fix, extends battery life for up to 14 hours and is intended for ground use such as exploring or camping. Finally, with the fourth mode—and this is pretty neat—by programming in your expected course, entering a simulated airspeed, and running the unit in the simulation mode, you can confirm that all waypoints will track as planned. The unit's portability makes it great not only for camping, but also for use in a boat or car.

The Garmin receiver is highly sensitive, which is necessary to receive the relatively low-strength satellite signals, and performs well even with a poorly installed antenna cabling system. Although I don't recommend a "coat hanger" antenna installation, this unit is so well designed that it will provide accurate course data even when conditions aren't optimum.

If space is at a premium, the Garmin GPS will fit a standard 6.25-inch by 2-inch panel cutout, but it is only 4 inches deep, so it's easy to squeeze into a tight panel space, especially if a torque tube or similar obstruction prevents deeper units from being installed.

During the Persian Gulf War, Garmin GPS units were fitted to French Jaguar jets and provided navigation data that allowed the French aircraft to maintain highly accurate positioning during battle conditions. This unit proved to be so accurate that when the aircraft was moved from its parking place to a distance 0.8 mile away, then back to the parking spot waypoint, the aircraft was only 6 inches away from its original position.

Magellan Systems

Magellan's SkyNav 5000 is a five-channel GPS receiver that offers a bright, readable, wide-angle display. Magellan calls its display "Ultraview" and says the display can be "easily seen day or night."

Unique features of the SkyNav 5000 include ability to store 1000 user waypoints along with waypoint messages entered by the user. Up to 20 flight plans with 20 waypoints per flight plan can be stored. With two standard RS-232 ports, the SkyNav 5000 can be interfaced with moving maps, fuel-management systems, altitude encoders, CDIs, HSIs, and autopilots.

II Morrow

II Morrow's new Apollo Nav Management System is the most impressive new offering in light-airplane avionics. In creating the Apollo NMS system, II Morrow, which is a division of United Parcel Service, is approaching this whole navigation ballgame from a different angle than most manufacturers. The Apollo NMC 2001 NMS system has multisensor capability and is designed to fit in the same size hole as a King KLN90 or Northstar M2. Data the Apollo NMS can accept includes navigation information from loran and GPS, fuel flow, and information from air data sensors.

The front panel features a three-line display and front-load data-card slot. With the five-channel GPS, air data, and fuel-flow sensor modules installed, the Apollo NMS will provide an abundance of information, including bearing, distance, track angle, groundspeed, time enroute, minimum safe altitude, time, fuel used, fuel remaining, fuel burn rate, outside air temperature, true airspeed, barometric altitude, winds aloft, rate of climb, and glideslope tracking.

A Dzus rail-mount version is also available, called the NMC 2001D. II Morrow also offers its low-cost Flybuddy GPS, a standalone five-channel GPS available with a worldwide database, 10-flight-plan storage, and 100 user-programmable waypoints. II Morrow's Flybuddy loran and GPS have been noted for their ease of use and reasonable cost.

Northstar

Northstar promised for some time to release a combined loran and GPS system, and it has, in the form of the IFR certifiable M2 loran with GPS sensor installed. The Northstar FliteCard database that is part of the M2 is shared by the loran and GPS sensors, therefore allowing the advantages of an international database for both loran and GPS.

Northstar developed this system as a six-channel multitracking system that updates every second. A standalone GPS is also available, called the GPS-600 Navigator, and it uses the same six-channel GPS sensor and FliteCard user-updateable database as the M2.

For Northstar M1 loran owners who want GPS capability without buying a new black box, Northstar offers the M2V field-retrofittable upgrade kit that incorporates the company's 8100A six-channel GPS sensor, bringing the M1 up to full GPS capability.

Trimble

Trimble has likened the advent of GPS to a new utility. Like the water or electrical distribution system that provides for our basic needs, GPS provides users a utility called *positioning*. This positioning utility is not only for military use but has virtually unlimited uses in the civilian arena. Campers, for example, who want to go wandering through the Rocky Mountains can use a hand-held GPS unit not much bigger than a pair of binoculars.

During the Persian Gulf War, foot soldiers had the security of knowing their exact positions even while in the middle of an unfriendly and hostile desert, thanks to their hand-held GPS units. Major trucking fleets have incorporated GPS for navigation and tracking, and the shipping company United Parcel Service even bought loran/GPS manufacturer II Morrow. (Eventually, the method for determining property lines could be as simple as tramping around with a portable GPS receiver.) Trimble reports that 135 of their NAV GPS receivers were sent to British forces during the Persian Gulf War. One British pilot was quoted as saying, "If we didn't have GPS, we'd still be in the Gulf because we'd be lost."

Trimble's current offerings include the TNL-2000 loran and TNL-3000 multisensor loran/GPS. The TNL-3000 is essentially the same as the TNL-2000, but by adding the GPS sensor it combines IFR-certifiable loran and the accuracy of GPS along with the ease of the front-loading Jeppesen NavData card update. Combining loran and GPS in one unit lends itself to easier future IFR certification.

With great accuracy, the Trimble GPS can calculate a bearing to any point on the earth, display the waypoint, its ground speed, track, estimated time enroute, vertical position, wind speed, safe altitudes, and it can drive a CDI needle on the HSI or stand-alone CDI. You get all this plus the data on the Jeppesen NavData card including VORs, intersections, NDBs, airspace boundaries, and MEAs.

For the executive crowd, Trimble also offers a stand-alone GPS receiver, the TNL-8000, designed to be fitted to existing long-range navigation systems such as VLF/Omega, to provide the most precise position, tracks, and velocity data possible. Six channels allow for continual tracking of up to eight satellites, automatically selecting the optimum combination to ensure accuracy of position and altitude within one second or less. The TNL-8000 can be interfaced, using the standard Arinc 429 databus, with long-range nav systems, flight management systems, and EFIS.

For those commercial aircraft that don't have Omega already installed, Trimble designed the TNL-7900, a combined VLF/Omega and GPS system that directly replaces older ARINC 599 systems. For smaller general aviation jets and executive aircraft, Trimble offers the TNL-7880. Optimized for low cost and weight and small size, the TNL-7880 provides flexible and reliable navigation through a combination of an older technology combined with state-of-the-art GPS. Information used for navigation is the more accurate of VLF/Omega or GPS.

The display on all three units is a seven-color CRT with eight lines of 14 characters, operated by a full alphanumeric keypad.

INSTALLATION TIPS

The best place for GPS antenna installation is on top of the aircraft's fuselage, as far forward as possible, but no closer than three feet from the windshield. GPS antennas aren't as sensitive to P-static as loran antennas. Because GPS relies on line-of-sight reception, any shading from vertical stabilizers or other obstructions can severely limit reception in certain directions. If you're installing GPS in a helicopter, make sure the installer guarantees, in writing, that the system won't be affected by the rotor blades or the vertical rotor shaft.

GPS antennas are usually flat, rectangular-shaped devices, but when the aircraft is sitting on the ground, standing water on flat antennas can decrease signal strength. You might consider an antenna with a raised, curved upper surface like Bendix/King's KA91 GPS antenna, or the antenna could be mounted at a slight angle to allow moisture to run off. Although any antenna should be bonded properly to its mounting place, it's not as critical with GPS antennas, and good reception has been demonstrated without the extra effort of antenna bonding.

Other than the above, installation procedures are similar to any radio. If rack-mounted, make sure the installer mounts the rack securely to the side rails using all four mounting fasteners. The harness exiting from the rear of the radio should be supported to prevent chafing and stress on connectors. The GPS wiring harness and coaxial cable should be routed away from heavy current sources and raw RF lines coming from other radios like coms, DME, and transponder.

GPS MANUFACTURERS

These GPS manufacturers' addresses can be found in the Sources section at the end of this book.

Arnav Systems

Bendix/King

Garmin

II Morrow

Magellan

Mid-Continent Instrument (GPS CDI)

Northstar Avionics

Trimble Navigation

HAND-HELD GPS MANUFACTURERS

See Sources section of this book for the addresses of these hand-held GPS manufacturers.

Evolution

Garmin

Magellan Systems

Sony

Trimble Navigation

15
Autopilots

AUTOPILOTS CAN BE AS SIMPLE AS A TURN COORDINATOR THAT PROVIDES information to drive an aileron servo for a simple wing-leveling system or as complex as an integrated flight management system that costs hundreds of thousands of dollars. The types most commonly installed in light airplanes are the wing-leveler and/or more sophisticated systems with altitude hold, glideslope capture, and complete nav tracking capability.

An autopilot consists of the following components:

- a controller with annunciators and buttons for pilot operation (what you see in the panel)
- an autopilot computer/amplifier (which manages and controls the signals that travel from the attitude-sensing devices such as attitude gyros, barometric sensors, and turn coordinators to the servos)
- and the servos, which translate the autopilot computer signals into action by moving the control surfaces, ailerons, elevator, rudder, and elevator trim

Servos are attached to control-surface control cables via bridle cables, which are short cables that run from the servo to the control-surface cable.

You've no doubt come across the term "axis" when reading about autopilots. Sometimes a wing-leveler autopilot is called a one-axis autopilot, and an autopilot that has aileron and elevator servos is called a two-axis autopilot, or sometimes three-axis if the autopilot controls elevator trim, too. Does that make an aileron, elevator, elevator trim, and yaw damper autopilot a four-axis autopilot? Perhaps, but the reason I mention this is just to warn you that the axis reference is by no means standardized, and for accuracy, you should find out what an avionics seller is talking about when they refer to autopilot axes. Don't just assume they mean aileron, elevator, and elevator trim servos when they talk about a three-axis autopilot.

AUTOPILOT GYROS

One of the more critical components of the autopilot system is the gyro that senses small changes in the airplane's attitude and feeds the information to the autopilot computer for correction to return the airplane to the desired course and altitude. Most autopilot systems use the attitude indicator or flight director for this information, although S-TEC's autopilot uses the turn coordinator and altitude information for sensing attitude changes. Century Flight Systems offers a simple wing-leveler autopilot that uses the turn coordinator, too.

Regardless of the attitude of the airplane (within certain limits), the gyro will stay erect in relation to the earth's horizon, sending compensating electrical signals only when the airplane's attitude changes. In order to do their job, these electrical signals must have muscle, and that is provided by the autopilot servos, which drive the airplane's control surfaces to correct any deviation.

The main gyro used in the autopilot system is usually either the flight director or the attitude indicator (or the turn coordinator in an S-TEC autopilot system). The difference between a flight director and a regular attitude indicator is that the flight director contains command bars that tell you, the pilot, what to do to stay on a selected flight path. Instead of commanding the autopilot to turn or climb to stay on course, the flight director is commanding the pilot. This saves you the trouble of having to interpret the data presented to you and allows you to concentrate on flying the airplane.

The gyro is the autopilot system's monitor, watching navigation receivers and its own attitude sensors for minute changes, then reacting and sending signals to the autopilot to make corrections in order to stay on the desired flight path.

Autopilot gyro installation tips

Being panel-mounted, the gyro requires a secure, trouble-free installation to prevent future mechanical and electrical failures. The installation must allow for easy viewing by pilots, G forces during landing, engine vibration, clearance for harnesses and plumbing, and ease of access to prevent shocks to the unit during removal and installation. Vendor installation manuals illustrate recommended installation methods; however, this might not satisfy a particular custom installation.

Typical flight director (top center).

More expensive flight management systems use remote gyros, which can be larger and thus provide better information to the autopilot. It's unlikely you'll see one of these in a light, piston-powered-airplane autopilot installation, however.

Autopilot gyro problems

Given the small amount of electrical current forming the nervous system of the autopilot, it isn't any wonder that the smallest error will affect the accuracy of its operation. Errors can occur from gyro failures due to bearing race breakdown, airflow restrictions due to kinked hoses or a contaminated vacuum system, incorrect mounting angle, high G force (a drop of only ¼ inch can result in up to a 20G force being applied to the gyro's sensitive bearings), poor instrument panel shock mounting, or electronic malfunction.

Gyro failure from internal wear usually doesn't occur until over 1000 hours. Bearing-to-race friction wear, inner or outer gimbal surface erosion, and heat all play a major part in internal gyro component failure. Sudden shocks such as bumps that could occur if the unit is banged around on a shop cart or during installation can shatter the jeweled movements or flatten bearings. Because proper operation of an air-driven gyro depends on an adequate flow of air, minute particles of dust, tobacco smoke, and other contaminants can clog vacuum filters and reduce efficiency.

Vacuum filters should be replaced per manufacturer recommendation. Usually the small foam filter on the vacuum regulator should be changed each 100 hours, and the large central canister filter should be changed every 500 hours or more frequently if people smoke in your airplane or you often fly in dusty, dry conditions.

Look for inaccurate indications on your attitude indicator including precessing, slow erection, spinning, or tumbling on shutdown. You'll usually spot excessive precessing shortly after powering up the gyro, but spinning or tumbling, caused by damaged or worn bearings, shows up when the gyro is spinning down after shutdown. Bearing damage could have been caused by improper handling during replacement or during maintenance under the instrument panel or by one too many a hard landing.

AUTOPILOT INSTALLATION TIPS

When considering a new autopilot, two of the companies you'll probably be looking at will be Century Flight Systems and S-TEC. Both offer modular systems that can be expanded upon, starting with a simple, relatively low-cost, single-axis, roll-control system and building up to a sophisticated, altitude-hold, navigation-coupled flight control system. My recommendation is to go with a modular system if you plan to keep the airplane for a while and want to add to its capabilities as you can afford to. Less expensive nonmodular autopilots are available, but they limit you to whatever you purchase at the time and can't be added to later on.

Enemies of the autopilot are heat, cold, vibration, poor wiring routing, and incorrect location. Avoid having the autopilot computer located next to the strobe power supply; the computer should also be at least ¼ inch away from other black boxes and any nearby structure. There should be enough slack in the wiring harness connected to the computer to allow easy removal, but not too much slack that the wiring just flops around and rubs on nearby metal. The harness should be supported 8 to 10 inches from the connector at the computer to prevent too much slack in the line.

If you are having an autopilot installed for the first time in your airplane and there isn't a standard place to put it (like the factory location for the Century autopilot on Pipers), consult with your installer about where you want the control head and annunciator lights located. Sometimes the ideal spot for the control head is on the center pedestal, behind the engine controls. Your installer might have to manufacture a bracket for that location, and care must be taken to prevent autopilot wiring from interfering with engine controls. The annunciator panel should be installed where you can see it easily. Many installers put it just above the flight director (or attitude indicator, as the case may be) but below the glareshield. The point here is, your input is important because you're the one who will be flying with this installation, so get involved during the process so that you'll have a better chance of a happy result.

Feedback and amplification circuits in the autopilot's control system are low voltage and susceptible to interference from extraneous signals caused by fluctuating power circuits and other radios, especially transmitters. These circuits are also referred to as sensitive circuits because they are sensitive to outside interference and must be protected to prevent accidental autopilot disconnect or other malfunctions. Normal use of shielded, twisted-pair wiring and proper bonding of all components will help assure the autopilot will be efficient and reliable, but keep in mind that the more complex the autopilot, the more potential areas of sensitive circuitry are installed and thus the more potential for introducing errors.

Before buttoning up the airplane after autopilot installation, go over all the cabling with your installer and watch the action of the autopilot cables as the autopilot is tested. It's very important that cables remain securely on their pulleys and capstans during autopilot operation, and none of the cables should come close to rubbing sides of feedthrough holes, wiring, structure, or brackets.

If, as is usual, the autopilot computer is installed in a remote spot in the airplane, make sure it is well protected from potentially harmful moisture and excessive heat. Don't just let the installer put it in the most convenient place. Find a spot that will contribute to the computer's longevity.

Autopilot problems

One of the most common autopilot problems is porpoising, which occurs when using the autopilot in altitude-hold mode. *Porpoising* is when the autopilot causes the nose of the airplane to hunt up, then down, roughly every 10 seconds, making any type of flying very uncomfortable. In most cases, porpoising can be relatively easy to correct because the usual cause is excessive slack in the flight control cables and autopilot bridle cables. You can prevent this problem by simply ensuring that your aircraft's cable tensions are kept within proper limits at your annual inspection.

Many forces act upon the airplane in flight, and if the control cable tensions are out of tolerance, the autopilot tends to overwork itself as it overshoots and undershoots its prescribed limits while attempting to correct for the incorrect travel. The autopilot's attempts to correct for loose cable tensions can reduce the life of the autopilot. Servos, cable guides, pulleys, and even autopilot electronics will be affected due to heat buildup and stress generated by the constant and relentless operation of the autopilot.

In one case, I discovered the cause of the porpoising to be a loose bridle cable, but it wasn't because of a lack of tension. The autopilot installer had used undersized rivets to hold a pulley bracket, so one end of the bracket moved every time the cable was tensioned and the system acted as though there was a lot of slack in the bridle cable. This customer was lucky—a simple replacement with stronger rivets solved the problem.

During a climb to a preselected altitude, slack cables will cause problems in establishing the correct altitude. After normally overshooting the preselected altitude, the autopilot attempts to recover to the correct altitude, but due to excess cable slack, it compensates improperly and the airplane levels out at an altitude higher than selected. The more slack, the worse the overshoot.

In another scenario, after a porpoising incident, we checked all cable tensions and found them within limits. The autopilot computer and servo checked okay, but the airplane still porpoised. At this point, we had to consider cold soaking as the cause of the porpoising. *Cold soaking* is where low ambient temperatures cause the aluminum airframe to shrink more than the steel control cables. The colder it gets, the looser the cables. The center section of some large twins can shrink up to a hundredth of an inch in cold air. This new slack in the control cables can confuse the autopilot and its sensors, causing porpoising and other problems. The trouble is difficult to track down because once on the ground in warmer temperatures, everything checks out okay. Some manufacturers compensate for this problem by adjusting control cable tensions to the high end of the recommended setting, especially for longer airframes that fly at high altitudes.

One way to prevent the cold-soaking problem is to have your aircraft's cable tensions set after the airplane has been sitting in a cold hangar all night. Even though you're not duplicating the effects of flying in cold air at high altitudes, the settings will be closer to providing the necessary cable tension than if the tensions are set in a warm hangar with the airframe expanded.

A rule of thumb used for preliminary tension checks calls for bridle cable tension at 50 percent of the primary control cable tension. Don't use this as a final setting; instead refer to the specification of the airframe and/or autopilot manufacturer. Once the airplane warms up again, it isn't a bad idea to recheck the tensions to make sure they don't end up out of tolerance as the temperature changes.

Once tensions are set, perform an operational test to evaluate autopilot function. Although pilots rarely experience problems with overtight cables, one symptom can be oscillation effects similar to porpoising, but with a more pronounced but shorter period (usually less than 10 seconds) between up-and-down cycles.

Slack cables can also cause problems in the lateral axis like overshooting of bank angle when using the heading bug to change heading while on autopilot. As the autopilot computer senses that the desired bank angle has been achieved (to give a standard-rate turn), the computer tells the roll servo to zero-out the ailerons, which should hold the airplane at the desired bank angle. The slack in the cables, however, causes a greater bank angle than that needed for a standard-rate turn.

The attitude indicator, sensing the error, will transmit a correcting signal to the autopilot servo. But the slack in the cables allows the servo to drive the ailerons to the incorrect position, once again followed by the attitude indicator's repeated sensing of the error. As this is a closed-loop system, the action continues, resulting in what is commonly known as "wing rock and roll."

Other elusive autopilot problems that cause porpoising and sloppy pitch and roll control or even undesirable Dutch rolling are usually traceable to contaminated connectors in the autopilot servos and computer. Assuming all cable tensions are correct, the next troubleshooting step is to carefully check all electrical connectors in the autopilot system.

One of the preventive measures I recommend to prolong autopilot health is periodic maintenance on the servos. Every year or 1000 hours, whichever comes first, it's a good idea to have the servo capstan assemblies removed and the cable clutch settings adjusted to vendor specifications. This is something that is usually ignored unless there is a problem, but by keeping the clutch settings optimal, you'll prevent a lot of problems and save money in the long run. After reinstalling the servo, recheck and adjust if necessary bridle cable tensions.

Here's another important maintenance tip: a lot of owners are having their airframes treated with ACF-50 corrosion-prevention fluid. The treatment consists of spraying the ACF-50 into every nook and cranny of the airframe for maximum corrosion prevention. It's been found, however, that the ACF-50 fluid can damage the material used on autopilot and trim servo clutches, so if you've having the ACF-50 treatment, make sure the facility covers your servo clutches before spraying.

AUTOPILOT TESTING

Your autopilot should have a manufacturer-recommended test procedure in the autopilot operational manual, and this is the test you should perform before any flight where you'll be relying heavily on the autopilot. You can also use this test as an initial troubleshooting test to track down where any problems are occurring, but its chief value lies in helping you find troublesome malfunctions before they crop up unexpectedly. While performing the test, check the failure monitors for each system as well. These include warning flags, or the audible tone that tells you the autopilot has been shut off.

Once you've engaged the autopilot during the testing, determine if the control wheel turns left or right with the respective autopilot commands. Check if the control wheel responds properly after receiving pitch commands from the autopilot.

Establish if the autotrim is trimming in the correct direction. To check this, allow the control wheel to relax and provide a pitch down command to the autopilot. Allow the control wheel to move forward, and after 3 to 5 seconds, the autotrim should run the trim in the down direction. Perform the same test in the up direction by applying a pitch up command to the autopilot, and confirm that the control wheel moves back and 3 to 5 seconds later the trim moves in the upward direction.

Here's how to check the autopilot override to confirm proper servo clutch settings. You need to be able to override the autopilot if it won't let go and for some bizarre reason you can't shut it off (highly unlikely). With the autopilot engaged, force the control wheel left and right. You should be able to override the autopilot in both the lateral and pitch axes. If you have a yaw damper installed, you should be able to override that too, using the rudder pedals. If you can't override any of these, you might have to have the servo clutches adjusted.

You'll have to simulate a yaw command for the yaw test. Your autopilot manual might suggest a method, but one way of doing this is to unscrew the attitude indicator from the panel and rotate it 25 degrees, which should simulate a roll crossfeed to the yaw damper system. Then determine if the rudder pedals are moving in the proper direction and that you can override the yaw system and stop the rudder travel.

One of the most important tests you can perform are the various methods of shutting off the autopilot. More than a few accidents have been caused by pilots panicking when the autopilot runs away with the trim and commands full nose-down trim, for instance, and the pilot tries to fight the controls to level the airplane. The more the pilot pulls back on the control wheel, the more the autopilot trims the nose down, and the only way the pilot can regain control is to shut the autopilot off and retrim the nose.

There are two types of control-wheel disconnects: one for disconnecting the autopilot, and one for disconnecting the electric trim in case of runaway trim. Runaway trim can occur in King autopilot systems if a certain transistor in the trim servo fails by short-circuiting while power is applied. This is a rare situation, but the trim disconnect switch is there if needed. Older systems used a two-detent disconnect switch. This first detent disconnects the autopilot, and the second detent disconnects the trim. If the switch is a new, one-detent type, both autopilot and trim will disconnect simultaneously when you push the button.

Autopilot trim switches and disconnect button (right).

In sophisticated autopilots, the entire autopilot should disconnect when you shut down the slaved compass system while in autopilot nav mode or if the compass system fails on its own. Test the autopilot disconnect switch on the yoke, the switch on the control head, the circuit breaker, and in a worst-case scenario, use the radio master or even the master electrical switch to shut the autopilot off. When you turn the power back on, of course, the autopilot should stay off, but it isn't a bad idea to check this because sometimes the autopilot on-off switch can stick in the "on" position.

With some autopilots, a horn will sound and a light activate when turning them off. On some older systems, depressing the test switch could disengage the autopilot, but this isn't correct, and some vendors offer modification kits to fix this. Refer to the autopilot's operating handbook for the many ways to shut off the autopilot, to learn the exact procedures, and practice doing them.

AUTOPILOT FLIGHT TESTING AFTER NEW INSTALLATION

Following installation, some adjustments might need to be made to your new autopilot. These tests can reveal adjustments that need to be made or problems you might have to get fixed.

When flying straight and level on autopilot, there should be no altitude gain or loss and no turning tendency. You shouldn't notice any pitch problems at the moment you engage the autopilot. When adjusting roll trim, the distance between each wing and the horizon is used as a reference, backed up by the turn coordinator. The compass is used as a reference to adjust the rudder trim if a yaw damper is installed.

With the autopilot engaged, check again for wings level, then engage altitude hold and monitor for any noticeable bumps, porpoising, or erratic movement. Bumps could indicate that the pitch-centering needs to be adjusted. If the autopilot is holding the chosen altitude, engage the heading mode and make sure the autopilot tracks the heading bug properly. Check for noticeable left or right wing dropping in tracking the heading bug, possibly an indication of the gyro needing rotational alignment.

Two other problems you might encounter with the heading bug could be due to the heading output from the heading indicator not being within tolerance. Or, the computed output of the flight computer might not be accurate. Except for wiring problems and electromagnetic interference, those are the two most common heading-tracking problems you'll run into.

If you notice that the autopilot isn't smoothly tracking in nav mode and following the CDI precisely, check the nav receivers first. The tracking of any signal by the autopilot is only as good as the quality of the signal received. To monitor the nav receivers, watch the CDIs while tracking a VOR without the autopilot. The CDI needles should be steady and shouldn't drift from left to right.

Warning: on some older King autopilots, if you test the marker beacons during an autopilot-coupled ILS approach, the autopilot will respond to the resultant gain reduction.

TROUBLESHOOTING CHECKLIST

This section lists some symptoms and their possible causes.

Hardover (nose pops up or down suddenly):
- ☑ Trim switch sticking
- ☑ Computer failure
- ☑ Wiring failure

Autopilot fails to respond to aerodynamic changes:
- ☑ Pickoffs in gyro open
- ☑ Open wiring between gyro and computer
- ☑ Defective gyro

Altitude-hold porpoising:

Divergent, gets worse and doesn't recover:
- ☑ Cable tension too loose
- ☑ Servo clutch slippage
- ☑ Defective servo

Damping, eventually recovers:
- ☑ Defective servo
- ☑ Insufficient current
- ☑ Noise injected into pitch circuitry

Control-wheel shudder:
- ☑ Broken wires
- ☑ Feedback circuitry failure (servo)
- ☑ Computer needs adjustment

Autopilot disengages by itself:
- ☑ Servo clutch torque set too high
- ☑ Flight control or bridle cable tension set too low
- ☑ Defective trim switch
- ☑ Defective trim servo
- ☑ Chaffing wires
- ☑ Defective disconnect switches

Autopilot constantly searching while nav tracking:

☑ Nav antenna or receiver problems

Autopilot drifts off heading while tracking heading bug:

☑ Trim knob not centered

☑ Flaps not centered or trimmed for straight-and-level flight

AUTOPILOT MANUFACTURERS

The following autopilot manufacturers' addresses can be found in the Sources section of this book.

Bendix/King

Brittain Industries

Century Flight Systems

Collins Avionics

Honeywell

S-TEC

Sigma-Tek

16
Transponders and collision-avoidance systems

TRANSPONDERS ARE LIKE DME IN THAT THEY ALSO ARE PULSE-TYPE avionics. Whenever a transponder is interrogated by a radar system, the transponder "replies" with a pulse of information containing the four digits that you have dialed in to the face of the transponder and, if equipped with an encoder, your altitude.

TRANSPONDER MODES

Mode A refers to the coded reply, the four digits that show radar controllers your position. *Mode C* shows not only the coded reply, but your altitude, too, helping controllers keep traffic in busy areas separated. Neither Mode A nor C is selective enough to provide sufficiently accurate information in busy airspace and can even cause erroneous display of near-midair collisions that never even happened.

Ground radars constantly sweep the skies, interrogating all airplanes within range. If the radar is sweeping a congested hub, such as Los Angeles International Airport and the airspace surrounding it, an enormous number of interrogations and replies are taking place. Because of the huge amount of traffic and short duration of time between the transmissions, transponder replies can overlap each other and confuse the ground radar. When flying close to radar sites, pilots of interrogated aircraft might have to set their transponder sensitivity to the "low" position to prevent false targets. Some pilots might forget to switch the transponder back to "high" and might get a call from ATC gently hinting them to "please recycle your transponder."

"Well, at least the transponder works!"

In the past few years, transponders have become increasingly important, especially after some rather unfortunate midair collisions occurred. The FAA now requires that pilots of airplanes that are transponder-equipped turn them on when flying in controlled airspace. After December 30, 1993, all aircraft flying within 30 nautical miles of the center airport of Class B airspace (TCA) must be equipped with Mode C capability to transmit altitude information to ground controllers along with the four-digit transponder code.

There is an ongoing regulatory attempt to mandate Mode S transponders. For Part 91 operators, the latest rule specified that after a certain date, only Mode S transponders could be installed. That rule is now on hold and, at least as of this writing, Mode C transponders were still being manufactured and installed.

If the time comes when you need a new transponder and the new rule takes effect again, you might want to hurry up and buy a Mode C transponder before they're outlawed. Mode S transponders are very expensive, and it doesn't look like the price will ever be as low as Mode C.

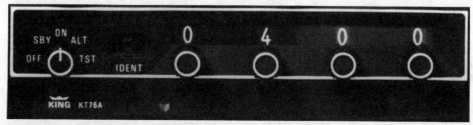

Bendix/King KT76A transponder.

Bendix/King KT79 solid-state transponder with encoding altimeter display.

One important note about Mode S transponders, when and if they ever become required: the transponders rely on a discrete code that is assigned exclusively to a particular airplane. So if you were having a Mode S transponder installed, you would have to make sure you were assigned a discrete code for your transponder at the same time. The FAA is concerned that Mode S transponders are being installed without discrete codes being assigned or using generic codes like all ones or zeros.

Encoders

There are two ways to provide altitude information along with your Mode A transponder code. The least expensive is to add a blind encoder or digitizer, which is a small aluminum box that can fit easily under the instrument panel. If you don't already have an altimeter or you'd like to have a spare altimeter, you can go the more expensive route of getting an encoding altimeter. This fits into a standard 3-inch hole in your instrument panel.

In either case, once you have a blind encoder or an encoding altimeter installed, the Mode C or "alt" setting on your transponder will allow you to fly within 30 miles of Class A airspace and into airports inside Class A airspace.

TRANSPONDER INSTALLATION TIPS

Because both DME and transponders are pulse-type equipment, transponders can suppress the DME signal (see chapter 12). Some avionics shops and factory installers wire the DME suppression protection into the system but don't hook it up. This leaves the owner the option of having it hooked up later if DME suppression becomes a problem. It's never a good idea to hook it up if there isn't a problem, however, because the feature can actually mess up DME operation.

I prefer and usually recommend the panel-mounted transponder because the remote installation means there's a lot of wiring from the instrument panel to the black box. If it's all the way in the back of the airplane, this means removing a bunch of upholstery and possibly introducing many areas of potential errors. One major hazard is piercing avionics wiring with upholstery screws when reinstalling upholstery.

Transponders operate at a frequency that isn't susceptible to the same interference problems that bedevil com, nav, ADF, and loran systems. To ensure no interference from other noise generators and P-static, however, it's important to install a properly bonded antenna on a 6- to 8-inch ground plane, free of interfering obstructions.

The transponder antenna is the short, little, blade type or the cheaper rod with a little ball on the end. As you might remember from chapter 12, the rod-type antenna is very sensitive to the long arm of the airplane washer and can be easily bent or damaged. I've seen cases where a mechanic who broke off the antenna simply stuck the rod back into the base, hoping no one would notice that it was broken. The transponder actually worked, until the rod fell out. Stick with the blade antenna; it will last longer and provide better service.

TRANSPONDER TESTING

There are three tests done on transponder systems:

- self-test
- FAA-mandated ramp test
- flight test

First, most transponders have a self-test function you can perform. On a King transponder, for instance, you turn the knob all the way to the right temporarily, then let the knob go. This causes the transponder to generate a simulated signal internally, lighting the reply light. This isn't much of a test, so don't absolutely rely on it to tell you if the transponder is really doing its job.

The second test is the FAA-mandated ramp test, required under FAR 91.413.

The final test is the flight test. This should be performed to evaluate overall operation and compatibility with other aircraft systems if this is a new installation. The transponder should provide a good signal at 6,000 to 12,000 feet at a range of 50 nautical miles from the ground radar. Your encoding altimeter or blind encoder should give your altitude plus or minus 125 feet at all times. Flying in a circle, the controller's radar should not take more than two sweeps without seeing your transponder.

Finally, you can fly a simulated surveillance approach down to 200 feet. The radar should not miss or drop your target during any given 10 sweeps during your low pass at 200 feet. These distances and altitudes are approximate because of the different power outputs of each manufacturer's transponder. Use these only as a guide to determine if your transponder is meeting minimum conditions.

COLLISION-AVOIDANCE SYSTEMS

Most manufacturers are making collision-avoidance systems compatible with the TCAS II (traffic alert and collision avoidance system) standard. TCAS-equipped aircraft provide pilots with traffic advisories and resolution advisories (advice on manuevers to avoid conflicts) on "threat" aircraft that might come too close or pose a midair collision threat. TCAS gets its information from threat-aircraft transponders. TCAS systems are very expensive and must include costly Mode S transponders, with some of the lower cost systems starting at over $40,000. TCAS I equipment, which gives only traffic advisories, but not resolution advisories, is currently under development and should be on the market in 1993. Mode S transponders are not needed in aircraft with TCAS I installed.

Ryan International, a company owned by Paul Ryan who designed and marketed the Stormscope before selling that company, designed the lower-cost TCAD (traffic alert and collision-avoidance device) system for light aircraft owners who want some measure of additional protection from crowded skies. TCAD also perceives threat aircraft via their transponder outputs, displaying threat aircraft range, but not threat aircraft bearing information.

A company called Flight Technology International offers the Airtrac moving-map/collision-avoidance system that displays threat aircraft that have the company's Airtrac system installed.

TRANSPONDER MANUFACTURERS

These transponder manufacturers' addresses are listed in the Sources section at the end of this book.

Aire-Sciences

Becker Avionics

Bendix/King

Collins Avionics

Narco Avionics

S-TEC

Sigma-Tek

Terra Avionics

ENCODER MANUFACTURERS (ALTIMETERS AND/OR BLIND ENCODERS/DIGITIZERS)

These manufacturers produce encoding devices; see Sources for addresses.

ACK Technology

Aero Mechanism

Aerosonic

Ameriking

Bendix/King

II Morrow (for II Morrow loran and GPS systems)

Kollsman

Narco Avionics

Pointer

Terra Avionics

Trans-Cal Industries

United Instrument

COLLISION-AVOIDANCE SYSTEM MANUFACTURERS

These companies offer collision-avoidance systems. See Sources for addresses.

Bendix/King

B.F. Goodrich Flight Systems

Collins Avionics

Flight Technology International

Honeywell

Ryan International

Trimble Navigation

17
Emergency locator transmitters

AN EMERGENCY LOCATOR TRANSMITTER (ELT) IS SIMPLY A TRANSMITTER designed to activate when subjected to a specified G load. ELTs transmit on 121.5 MHz for civilian reception and 243.0 MHz for military reception. There are some new regulations for ELT design that you should know about, and some features that new units offer that you might want to consider if you are buying a new ELT.

ELTs frequently are forgotten about or ignored because they don't do anything except after a crash landing or if someone has accidentally left one on. Unfortunately, while ELTs have saved many lives, they also cause a lot of false alarms and unnecessary expenditure of search-and-rescue effort. In 1991, nearly 97 percent of all ELT signals were reportedly false alarms. Furthermore, a 1990 NASA study showed that in 75 percent of the 3,270 general aviation accidents that happened between 1983 and 1987, the ELT didn't even activate.

The National Transportation Safety Board, in a recommendation to the FAA, suggested that current ELTs are lacking in that they don't transmit on the international search-and-rescue satellite frequency of 406 MHz. The international satellite system can detect ELTs broadcasting on 121.5 or 243.0 MHz; however, it requires an additional pass by the satellite, delaying possible rescue. There is a TSO for 406-MHz ELTs (TSO C126), but there hasn't been a rush to build these units, probably because they cost much more to build, although Artex does offer one.

NTSB also recommended that FAR 43, Appendix D be amended to require mandatory periodic inspections of ELTs. This would include physical inspection of mounting, batteries for corrosion, antenna, wiring, G switch, and testing of the ELT's frequency alignment. Currently, the only requirement is that the ELT be working and that batteries be changed periodically.

TSO C91A applies to current ELTs and has standards for better G switches, antenna tethers, and stronger housings, which should reduce the amount of false alarms. All new ELTs must meet TSO C91A.

Artex now manufactures the ELS-10 ELT system, which it purchased from Arnav Systems. The ELS-10 interfaces with many loran and GPS systems and not only transmits the standard ELT signal, but also the location of the downed aircraft, based on loran or GPS information.

ELT REGULATIONS

FAR 91.207 gives pilots some relief for an ELT that needs to be removed for repairs. Most people misinterpret 91.207 to read that they can only fly their airplane within a 50-mile radius with the ELT removed. That, however, isn't the case.

First, 91.207 permits ferrying of newly acquired airplanes without ELTs to a place where the ELT is to be installed or ferrying an airplane with an inoperative ELT to a repair shop where it can be fixed. Here's the 50-mile rule: an airplane used for flight-training operations conducted entirely within a 50-nautical-mile radius of the airport where the training operations take place need not have an ELT installed at all.

Now here's the rule for ELTs removed for repair: FAR 91.207 (e)(10) states that for up to 90 days, an aircraft can be operated without its ELT, provided the aircraft records (logbook) contain an entry that includes the date of initial removal, make, model, and serial number of the ELT, and reason for removal. In addition, a placard must be installed within view of the pilot, stating "ELT not installed."

Thus, you can still operate your airplane normally while the ELT is being sent out for repairs. Don't forget that this removal can only be done by a licensed mechanic or under supervision of a licensed mechanic.

INSTALLATION TIPS

The criteria for ELT installation are somewhat specific. The ELT must be located somewhere in the aft fuselage where it can be securely mounted and the likelihood of the ELT surviving a crash is greatest. If existing shelving isn't available for mounting the ELT, the bracket provided with it can usually be mounted directly to the fuselage structure. The Narco ELT-10, used on Pipers for many years, is riveted directly to the aft fuselage skin, and that has proven to be a successful location. Wherever the ELT is mounted, the installation must allow the ELT to face in the proper direction, as marked on the ELT by a big arrow. Usually the ELT faces forward, but there are some vertically mounted ELTs as well. This is important for proper operation of the ELT's G-switch. If this is a new installation, consider installing it closer to the cockpit, perhaps behind the baggage compartment, so you can reach the ELT from inside the airplane and get to it quicker in case of an accident.

However the rack is installed, make sure it is properly bonded to the airframe. This means you need good metal-to-metal contact between the skin and the bracket. Also recommended is corrosion treatment of the bare metal, preferably with Alodine solution, before bracket installation.

The ELT's on/off/arm switch must be accessible to the pilot through an access panel that can be easily removed. In most cases, the access panel is held on by screws, so you should carry a straight-slot and Phillips-head screwdriver with you in the airplane at all times. Also, new installations are now required to have a remote ELT switch in the cockpit. Most ELT's are already wired for this; it's just a matter of hooking it up and installing the wiring and the switch in the cockpit.

Because the ELT depends on the external antenna for efficient transmission of emergency signals, make sure the antenna is bonded properly to the airframe. Anything getting in the way of good metal-to-metal contact between the base of the antenna and the airframe, like rubber gaskets, corrosion, or paint, can cause inefficient antenna operation. ELT antenna bases are usually made of stainless steel, so it's doubly important that the area where it will be mounted be treated with Alodine to prevent dissimilar metal corrosion between the steel antenna and aluminum skin. Watch this area during your preflights, because it will corrode eventually, and clean up the corrosion before it becomes bad enough to hamper operation of the antenna.

To bond the antenna to the airframe, remove paint and any corrosion in an area $\frac{1}{16}$-inch larger than the antenna hole. Clean the antenna base and corrosion proof the area around the hole with Alodine treatment. Install the antenna and check for resistance between the antenna base and the airframe of 0.0025 Ω or less. Note, you might need someone else to tighten the nut inside the airframe while you hold the antenna, or vice versa.

After the antenna is installed, apply a bead of silicone sealant around the antenna base. Hold the sealer nozzle at a 70-degree angle to the skin and move the tip backwards to help prevent air bubbles from forming under the sealant. Then smooth the sealant down using your fingers or a small spatula to obtain a consistent 45-degree slope from the antenna base to the skin. The sealant should cover the area of paint you cleaned off.

If the antenna is installed on a contoured area, you might have to use a gasket. In this case, you'll have to add metal, bonding washers that can reach through the gasket to make contact with the skin. Another alternative is an alclad gasket, made of soft aluminum that will form to the contour when you tighten the antenna down. Don't discard any gaskets that the vendor requires be installed with the antenna.

Typical ELT antenna installation.

With some antennas the mounting bases are nonconductive, and vendor supplied conductive foam gaskets are required.

ELT antennas are best located at least 3 feet from other antennas. On Piper Navajos and some other aircraft, the ELT is located inside the dorsal fin, which allows RF to pass through without hindrance and provides good protection from weather conditions that could harm the ELT. Wherever it is located, it should never be exposed to the elements.

Because ELTs operate on so few frequencies, they need only have an inexpensive whip antenna, usually provided with the ELT. If your antenna breaks, which isn't unusual, make sure you buy the antenna specified for your ELT, not just any old antenna that fits the existing hole.

BATTERY REPLACEMENT

Every time I've shown an owner what their ELT battery looks like, they always ask why they cost so much. The battery packs generally look like a bunch of D-cell alkaline batteries wired together. Essentially, that is what they are, except they are wired a special way that is approved by the FAA and that allows the batteries to have a two- to three-year operational life in your ELT.

The only way to assure high reliability of ELT batteries is for the battery manufacturer to procure raw batteries and weld all connections to form a dependable battery pack. All cells are mated into one unit using nickel-plated straps, and the entire assembly is inserted into a plastic case or mold-epoxied to prevent relative movement between individual cells. Teflon wires are soldered to the positive and negative terminals of the battery pack, and high-quality AMP or Molex mating connectors are attached for connecting the battery to the ELT.

Shelf lives for batteries vary, depending on type of battery used, design of the battery pack, and quality control during assembly. The alkaline cells used by ELT battery manufacturers have about a six-year shelf life, but for replacement purposes, FAA cuts that down by half, to a maximum of three years. You'll find you can buy either two- or three-year battery packs for your ELT.

When buying a new ELT battery, check the replacement date marked on the battery. If you bought a two-year battery, your new battery should have a solid two years left. Don't accept a battery whose life is already short by a few months.

To change the ELT battery, you must first remove the ELT from the airplane. Remember, this is something you can do only under the supervision of a licensed mechanic. Open the ELT access panel, making sure at the same time that the panel is easy to open. You don't want to find out that the corroded screws on the access panel won't come off the day you have a survivable accident.

Before attempting to remove the ELT, turn the on/off/arm switch to the "off" position. You could easily activate the ELT by removing it if you left the switch in the "arm" position. The ELT is usually held on its bracket by a simple clip; this is used on Narco's popular ELT-10, found on most Pipers. Many Cessnas have the Dorne and Margolin ELT installed, and this is held on by four Phillips-head screws. Cessna usually mounts its ELTs on the upper fuselage just aft of the baggage compartment.

To complete the removal of the ELT, you'll have to unscrew or disconnect any wires that go to the remote switch and the antenna coaxial cable. Don't mix up the remote wires, and mark them if you're not sure you'll be able to tell where they go back on. Note that on the ELT-10, there is a little plastic tab that sits between the ELT's own portable antenna (the flat, bendy metal strap wrapped around the antenna) and the ELT's plastic body. This tab, usually attached to the main antenna coax, must be installed between the portable antenna and the ELT whenever the main antenna is attached. That way, the portable antenna is disabled when the main antenna is attached, but if the unit is removed, the portable antenna is automatically connected, and all you have to do is extend the antenna strap and you can transmit as well as you could with the main antenna in the airplane. This is useful if you have to leave the airplane and want to take the ELT with you.

ELT TESTING

According to the FAA Airman's Information Manual, testing of ELTs, if necessary, should be done at five minutes past the hour and for a maximum of three audible sweeps. Testing at the wrong time and for too many sweeps could lead to unnecessary search-and-rescue efforts, so keep testing to a minimum.

There are two tests that you can perform. The first is to tune your radio to 121.5, then flip the ELT switch to the "on" position, then "off" after you've heard three or fewer sweeps.

The second test is to make sure the G switch is working and the ELT switch is in the "armed" position. Again, have your radio tuned to 121.5 MHz. Holding the ELT firmly, quickly move the ELT in a horizontal plane in the direction of the arrow printed on the ELT's body. Stop the movement suddenly in order to impose a G load on the ELT. This should set off the ELT. Shut the ELT off before more than three sweeps are heard. Don't try to test the G switch by whacking the ELT—it's not good for the unit's electronics.

Do not forget to leave the ELT with its switch in the "armed" position after reinstalling it. Otherwise it won't go off in a crash.

ELT REPAIRS

Usually the best place to get an ELT fixed is by the original manufacturer. Manufacturers offer reasonable turnaround time and also check the ELT for any other problems or updates that might be necessary.

ELT MANUFACTURERS

These ELT manufacturers' addresses are listed in the Sources section of this book.

ACK Technology
Artex Aircraft Supplies
Dorne and Margolin
Emergency Beacon
Narco Avionics
Pointer

18
Radar systems

MORE AND MORE SMALL AIRPLANES ARE SHOWING UP WITH RADAR already installed, and some even feature both radar and electrical-discharge-detecting 3M Stormscopes. Radar is still much more expensive than the Stormscope and costs more to maintain, too, with moving parts like antenna bearings and that wear out and other expensive components like waveguides and magnetrons.

All radars have included the following basic components.

- **Indicator.** This is what you look at for weather information. It is basically a CRT screen sized to fit your particular installation.
- **Receiver-transmitter (RT).** This includes the magnetron that generates the X-band radar signal and the circuitry that evaluates the returned signals and drives the indicator display.
- **Waveguide.** The radar signal must travel through the waveguide to reach the antenna. The waveguide is like a high-tech pipe through which the X-band signal flows, and it is necessary because regular wire cannot carry the signal.

- **Antenna.** The antenna sends the radar signal to the target, usually raindrops in a cloud, and collects the signals as they return from the target for processing by the RT.
- **Radome.** This provides an aerodynamic cover for the antenna that is transparent, or nearly so, to radar signals.

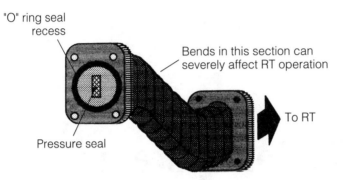

Because the radar signal frequency is outside the range of the signals that can be carried by wires or coaxial cable, a waveguide is used to channel the high-frequency RF from the receiver/transmitter to the antenna. The reflected signal returns to the antenna, through the waveguide, and into the receiver/transmitter.

RADAR ANTENNAS

The radar antenna, whether mounted in the nose of a light twin or in a pod under the wing of a single-engine airplane or even in the leading edge of the wing, is a complex piece of equipment. When equipped with gyro stabilization, the antenna rotates up and down and side to side to compensate for the pitching and rolling of the aircraft, thus keeping the same area in radar view, within limits, as the airplane turns and climbs. Without gyro stabilization, the radar antenna still moves as commanded by the pilot, and during all this movement, RF energy travels from the RT to the antenna through the waveguide then out to the target. After arriving at the moisture-laden clouds, the RF energy is reflected back to the antenna, travels through the waveguide and into the RT, where the radar display shows the pilot what lies ahead.

All of this action is dependent on the correct action of resolvers, motors, relays, and amplifiers. Should any contaminants such as moisture, dirt, or other corrosive contaminates enter the RT or the driving gear and motors, the radar's operation will become erratic or simply fail altogether. Proper preventive maintenance will prevent contaminates from affecting radar operation.

Most radar antennas used on general aviation aircraft today are the flat-plate, phased-array, radiator type. The power efficiency of the flat-plate antenna is significantly greater than the parabolic antenna due to lower side-lobe loss. Power from the RT is distributed to the right and left sections of the antenna, to be dispersed through slots in the antenna. The slots are slanted at varying angles from the centerline of the waveguide. The RF energy is "guided" from the waveguide through the rear of the antenna. As the energy passes through the slots in the antenna, there is a phase shift, but each slot has an opposing slot that acts to rephase the energy. The RF emerging from the front of the antenna is in phase, and accordingly, so will be the reflected signal.

Parabolic antennas are still used in larger commercial aircraft because for the size of the antenna, the weight is less than it would be for a comparable-size flat-plate antenna. Less tilt is needed for ground mapping with a parabolic antenna, plus the larger the parabolic dish, the greater the efficiency advantage over flat-plate antennas. A flat-plate antenna will still operate with dents or dings around the edges, but if a parabolic antenna is dented, the radiated efficiency can be drastically reduced.

RADOME

The radome is a streamlined, RF-invisible cover designed to protect the radar antenna while presenting as streamlined a profile to airflow as possible. Because the radome is made of materials like Fiberglas, which radio waves can pass through without hindrance, radomes are more sensitive to abrasion and cracking than a comparable metal surface. It is important to inspect radomes regularly for cracking and delamination to prevent premature failure, which could allow moisture to enter the radar antenna and damage moving parts or the radar itself.

Radomes are tuned to radar frequencies and "tweaked" for beam-to-wall incidence angle. The tweaking is essentially designing the walls of the radome to handle structural loads but still allow radar beams to escape and enter with minimum loss of efficiency. Although the thickness of the radome might not seem excessive, remember that the radar beam exits at an angle. This angle could cause the beam to have to travel through a thickness four times that of the actual thickness of the radome wall.

Not all radomes are round cones found on aircraft noses. You'll see small radomes on wing-mounted radar pods on high-wing single-engine aircraft like Cessna's 210 and turbine-powered Caravan. On Piper's single-engine piston-powered Malibu, the radome is actually part of the leading edge of the wing, and it is protected by a portion of the deicer boot. Interestingly, Goodyear, the manufacturer of the deicer boot, makes a boot out of a special type of rubber for the right wing of the Malibu that is more suited to efficient radar transmission. This boot is different enough from the "normal" type of boot used on the left wing that after a few years of operation, you can spot the difference in wear and tear between the left and right wing deicer boots on a Malibu. The left boot, after about five years, will have lots of cuts and pinholes and patches, while the right boot will look relatively clean.

Radome problems

Improperly designed or repaired radomes can set up superfluous reflections, causing undesirable side lobes of radar energy to radiate from the antenna. Naturally, these undesirable reflections occur at the worst possible time, causing random and less-than-accurate returns during adverse weather and increasing pilot workload. Because reductions in radar efficiency could be a result of radome problems, technicians might be unable to duplicate the problem. This might leave you with an ineffective radar just when you're trying to avoid a thunderstorm. Don't ignore the radome as a source of possible radar trouble.

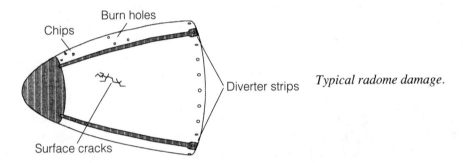

Typical radome damage.

You can check your radar system by performing a simple ground-map test. At a distance of 100 miles, the radar screen, when you have the antenna tilted down to map the ground, should show normal display of ground features to the left, right, and directly ahead of the airplane's path. Irregular display scans or dead portions of the scan might indicate a problem with the antenna system or radome. What is important to remember is that the radome is as much a part of the radar system as the RT or CRT. If the radar system can't be easily pinpointed as the cause of the problem, then the trouble is most likely in the radome. The easiest way to rule out a suspected radome is to ship it to an authorized radome repair facility, especially for a radome that has been in use for a long time without repair. In fact, the repair facility might find other problems with the radome that you weren't even aware of, so be prepared for that possibility.

Too often the radome is taken for granted. Everything from small stones to birds have their way with the radome. Receiving a torrent of aerial contamination, the composite radome is abused over and over. Many times this "normal" wear and tear creates a potential failure point, through which moisture can enter and freeze at altitude. As this takes place, the bonded layers of Fiberglas weaken until they delaminate.

During scheduled inspections such as annuals, these bruised areas are often overlooked or ignored because of cost considerations. Although the customer should be apprised of the damage, many times they aren't and the damage remains. Or when the owner is told about the problem, repairs might be put off because of high costs. Contributing to the problem is that ground personnel frequently push on radomes when moving airplanes. And finally, add to that wear and tear from radome removal for radar and other nose-mounted avionics maintenance.

During your preflight inspections, make it a habit to look closely at the radome. The earlier you find a damaged radome, the sooner you'll be able to get it fixed and keep the radar in top operating condition. Be especially alert for unreported damage that has been repaired incorrectly. Radome repair is an exacting and detailed field, and not just any mechanic can repair radomes properly. Unfortunately, there have been cases of radomes that were damaged during ground handling or being repaired incorrectly, causing poor radar operation. Some of the evidence to look for of improper repairs includes discoloration, deformation, large concave areas, and cracking.

Here is what mechanics should look for when inspecting a radome during a routine annual inspection:

- Scuffing, chipping, peeling, or painted surface
- Surface cracks (microcracking in composite material)
- Low areas, especially where surface cracks are evident in circular patterns
- Damaged mounting holes (Fiberglas torn)
- Water oozing from cracks (water has entered fiber core)
- Lightning-strike diverter damage
- Bonding strips damaged
- Excessive erosion wear
- Small pinhole-sized burn marks
- Poor paint job, signs of cratering, or pinholes
- Color change of erosion/static coatings from black to brown
- Plastic erosion cap improperly installed

If damage has occurred, look for signs of water contamination. This might look like a white, crusty trace or black streamers radiating away from a source of air flow. The white, crusty trace is mineral deposits left after water evaporates, and these deposits are especially bad for antenna bearings. The black streamers are a combination of oil and dirt, also not a good lubricant for moving parts. Failure to inspect regularly for this type of damage could result in failure due to corrosion.

Radar efficiency depends on a tight, narrow pulse of intense electromagnetic energy leaving the antenna, arriving at a target, and being reflected back to the antenna. If the energy is prematurely reflected, diffused, and spread out as it leaves the radome, a weaker return is the result, and the pilot gets erroneous information on the radar screen. Should water get trapped between laminated areas of the radome, it will effectively block the radiated signal as it leaves the antenna and attenuate the signal when it returns from the target.

Detection of trapped water is difficult, especially when it comes and goes as the temperature of the radome changes with altitude. Few shops have the equipment on hand to check for moisture contamination, although certified radome repair shops check for moisture as a normal part of a repair.

One mistake to watch for happens during repainting. Some paint shops apply striping along the side of the fuselage, terminating in a neat, narrow taper at the front of the nose, on the radome. Besides presenting a thicker path to the radar signal, these stripes frequently contain metallic particles, for that distinctive "look," which can easily reflect or diffuse radar signals. The distortion caused by the degraded signals could be extreme enough to show up on the radar screen.

Another painting mistake is failing to remove the original paint and just painting over the existing radome. The added paint layer can radically decrease signal efficiency. Even removing the old paint for repainting is a delicate operation. One wrong swipe with a sanding block, and too much of the radome material can be removed. This material must be replaced to retain the radome's design configuration and aerodynamic shape.

Your best bet when having your radar-equipped airplane repainted is to find out if the shop knows exactly how to handle radomes. If not, have your radome sent out for overhaul while your airplane is being painted, and tell the radome shop what colors are being used on your airframe so it can match the colors if this can be done without degrading the radome's performance.

Scuff marks on the radome are usually an indication of items striking the radome in the air or while taxiing on poor surfaces, or from hangar rash. "Hangar rash" is the nickname for mishandling of the airplane on the ground that results in dings and nicks and scrapes from running into hangar walls, other aircraft, or equipment. Don't be too worried about scuff marks on the radome unless other signs of damage are also visible. If scuff marks are accompanied by circular cracking, try pushing gently on the center of the circular area. If the section pops inward, there's a good chance the outer surface of the radome is damaged, and it needs to be inspected closer.

Paint chipping is usually the result of impact from ice or birds, from heat buildup from static charges, or poor paint application. When you spot paint damage such as chipping or peeling, have it repaired quickly. Delaying such repairs could allow moisture entry and freezing in the Fiberglas radome. Like the small nick in an auto windshield, paint damage can develop into far greater damage than originally suspected. Small pits or nicks from sand or other fine particles can be filled with a clear acrylic paint until more complete repairs can be made.

When humidity is low, static electricity discharge tends to occur. As air moves across the surface of the radome, electrons are stripped off the air molecules, leaving a negative charge. Often this charge is quite high and can cause radio problems or even damage to the radome's paint as the charge attempts to leave the radome and migrate to the airframe or into the atmosphere. This problem is most prevalent on high-speed aircraft such as heavy turboprops and jets.

To minimize the static problem, antistatic/antierosion coatings are applied to the nose of radomes. Although these coatings reduce the effects of static, they don't eliminate the problem. The black coating should last at least two years; after that the coating will turn gradually from black to brown, at which time it should be replaced by an authorized facility. Recommended coatings are either a black neoprene or polyurethane. Of the two, polyurethane is the best because it has very good antistatic and antierosion capabilities while retaining reasonable transmission efficiency.

Erosion caps are an alternative to paint-type coatings. These look like giant, soft contact lenses and are made of a thin film of formed polyurethane with an adhesive backing. Erosion caps have virtually no resistance to radar beams. The thicker, solid plastic caps aren't a good idea because it is difficult to obtain positive cap-to-radome contact, and this could allow moisture to get trapped behind the cap, degrading the radar signals.

Lightning-strike diverter strips are an important radome component and should be inspected regularly. The heat generated within the nose cone by a lightning strike can be enough to blow the nose apart. Diverter strips carry charges away from the nose to the airframe. Although lightning can be destructive, much of the damage can be reduced if diverter strips are solidly bonded to the airframe. Static wicks are available that can handle both static discharge and lightning.

Radome repairs

The simplest type of radome repair is injecting resin into pinholes caused by static burns. Technicians use a hypodermic needle to inject epoxy polyester into the hole and to fill open areas around the hole. At the same time, any carbon residue from the burn is removed because any leftover residue could act as a conduit for electrical charges, causing more damage. Adding too much resin can affect radar performance, so with this and any other radome repair, you should take it to a radome expert.

While composite repair principles apply to radomes, at least insofar as they are made primarily of composite materials, the tooling, experience, and skills to return the radome to original design configuration aren't found in most FBOs. Specialized radome repair shops have equipment for detecting moisture contamination, and after repairing a radome, these shops test the radomes to ensure they are within design limits for efficient radar transmission. All this equipment and expertise doesn't come cheap, but it's worth it to make sure your radome is providing the best protection for your radar antenna and optimum transmissibility for the radar beams.

Here is a case where lack of attention to proper radome repair might have been a factor in a fatal accident. It involved a twin on an instrument flight whose pilot was relying on radar to avoid severe weather. In reality, a severe weather front with huge thunderstorms lay directly in the pilot's flight path, but it seems that the pilot didn't spot the severe weather on the radar. The pilot was well qualified in the aircraft and its radar system and knew better than to try to fly through a storm of that magnitude. It can only be speculated that the pilot was totally unaware of the storm's intensity and proximity and was well into it before being able to turn away. But how did this happen to a conscientious pilot?

The answer could lie in what occurred earlier. While the airplane was being towed out of its hangar, it struck a tug, severely damaging the front of the thin-walled radome. A field repair was performed on the radome and the airplane was returned to service. What the pilot didn't know was that the radar system would display returns from the left and right of the airplane fine, but would indicate less weather than was actually there directly in front of the aircraft. Two flights later, the airplane came raining out of a thunderstorm in pieces. Was the repair at fault? It's up to you to decide, but consider also the question, "Is an unauthorized repair worth the risk?"

The world of radomes is quite complicated. Even the original specifications issued by the Radio Technical Commission for Aeronautics are being modified because of differing opinions about transmission standards. A new spec for radomes is being written, with two separate classes:

- type A, predictive windshear
- type B, covering conventional weather radar

Because radar manufacturers are motivated to provide the customer with the most power possible with easy-to-interpret displays, they are requiring that radomes meet the highest possible specifications. Honeywell, for example, requires a maximum 10-percent transmission loss for radomes to be used with its radars.

INSTALLATION TIPS

Vibration is an enemy of radar. The radar must not be mounted too close to the aircraft's skin; otherwise, damage could be caused by the buffeting of the skin against the radar. High-frequency vibrations can be created by odd combinations of bracketing and shelf attachment but can be avoided if the radar is properly mounted using vendor-recommended installation procedures and the correct hardware.

Corrosion and moisture contamination

Radar's worst enemy is moisture, which causes corrosion. Corrosion is normally the result of poor design, installation, or maintenance and can cause expensive problems, sometimes in the range of thousands of dollars.

The RT and its magnetron, the power supply, circuit boards, antenna bearings, and attaching hardware are all subject to failure from corrosion. Corrosion causes increased resistance in electrical connectors and printed circuit board contacts, drastically altering the operating parameters and overloading critical circuits. In addition to electronic failures, water and other contaminates can enter the antenna drive bearings, reducing their efficiency and causing eventual failure if preventive action isn't taken.

The evidence you're looking for is a black, graphite-colored substance and a white mineral deposit, which is a combination of oil, moisture, and dirt particles. The white mineral deposit is an indication that water has recently evaporated, leaving behind a crust-like substance that will act more like an abrasive than a lubricant, especially when it gets into antenna drive bearings. Moisture is a killer, especially when it acts as a transportation agent for hybrid contaminates such as oil, metal filings left over from a sloppy installation, dirt, and other corrosive elements than can attack the circuitry within the radar or cause temperature shock as it comes in contact with electronics operating at high temperatures.

Waveguides must be kept clean and dry. Pressurized aircraft usually have provisions for pressurized air to be ported to the waveguide. This helps the waveguide operate more efficiently at high altitudes. But because pressurized air is frequently full of moisture, it is necessary to keep desiccant materials in the waveguide to absorb moisture. The desiccant should be replaced periodically.

RADAR PROBLEMS

Radar problems come in a confusing variety, and correct interpretation will help you narrow the problem down so you can save money on troubleshooting and get right to the source of the problem. This section describes some of the most common problems.

CRT is not painting, the screen periodically shows only one sweep mark, it paints a scrambled screen, or it displays a target, then erases it. This could be a memory problem, or the radar might not be updating.

If the target is displaced after each sweep, say ¼ inch, the radar could be out of sync, but it is still attempting to update. Multiple targets and/or sweep lines might also be displayed with this problem.

If the scope isn't displaying weather, try initiating the test function by selecting test mode.

If a test pattern is present, this indicates the data lines are intact, the system trigger is presently arriving at the RT, and the four color levels are being correctly processed.

If there is no test pattern, look for an error in the system trigger circuitry.

If the CRT doesn't light up, expect the problem to be in the RT. If the CRT does light up and the range marks and alphanumeric symbols are being displayed but no test pattern is evident and the scope isn't painting weather, then look for system trigger failure.

If the radar is transmitting and "spokes" are being displayed on the screen, the automatic frequency control (AFC) could be unlocked. The presence of the spokes indicates the transmitter is transmitting, but because the AFC is unlocked, only intermittent reception of the incoming RF is processed, only when that RF is within the frequency of the receiver. The fault most likely lies in the magnetron not being within its designated frequency range (most magnetrons generally must fall within a frequency range of plus or minus 35 MHz).

When an antenna problem develops, it might show up as a jerky update sweep, smeared targets, or azimuths being clipped and only painting one side. When the sweep reference is passing center (the bore sight), it updates itself. If the bore is out of adjustment, then "catch up" occurs, causing a smeared image. If the bore sight isn't calibrated correctly, it needs to be matched to the radar indicator's sweep line.

Sophisticated radars have a gyro-stabilization system that keep the radar horizontal even if the aircraft rolls. Proper orientation of the roll gyro for the radar's antenna stabilization system is critical for accurate radar scanning. If the radar is displaying strange patterns while rolling and pitching the aircraft, see if the patterns disappear when the airplane is held in a straight-and-level attitude. If so, this could indicate a failure of the stabilization system.

If the radar scope displays excess ground clutter, either evenly centered or in the lower right or left corners of the screen, the antenna might require physical adjustment or there could be a gyro stabilization error if a stabilization system is installed. The gyro may be mispositioned or could have failed electronically. The stabilization gyro must be aligned with the aircraft in the inflight straight-and-level attitude and be positioned correctly fore and aft. Don't overlook the fact that the tilt adjustment could have been set too low, which would cause the radar to scan the terrain and cause the evenly centered ground clutter. This is an operational problem, not something wrong with the radar. For the problem where the radar paints one side or the other, you might suggest the technician perform a functional test on the gyro. If the gyro is replaced, expect the shop to perform a full radar stabilization alignment on your aircraft.

If the CRT paints red all the time, look for a defect or misalignment of the tilt drive.

Scrambled displays during communication transmissions aren't common. If you experience this problem, it could be caused by poor harness routing, open shielding, and poor bonds. The first step is to try to isolate the problem by temporarily substituting com coax cables with known good test cables. Or try switching com 1 coax with com 2 coax. If the problem moves to the second com, the problem is in the com antenna and/or coax cable. Bonding of the com antennas, instrument panel, the radar indicator, and installation of shielded wire are other steps that should help solve this kind of problem. The problem could be the radar indicator itself. It could be missing modifications that are designed to prevent the high-gain section of the radar from picking up extraneous RF from the com radios. If this is the case, it should be easier to simply have the radar indicator brought up to date instead of messing with coax and bonding and shielding, not that those factors shouldn't be done properly to start with.

Don't forget the corrosion problems mentioned earlier. If you spot any corrosion, make sure it's taken care of right away before it causes radar problems.

SAFETY

There is much that pilots and technicians need to know about proper radar operation, and one of the best ways to learn about radar is Archie Trammel's radar seminars. For more information on seminar dates and costs, contact AGT, Inc. at RD 1 500 Rosemary Drive, Trinidad, TX 75163. The phone number is (903) 778-2177.

RADAR MANUFACTURERS

These radar manufacturers' addresses are in the Sources section at the end of this book.

Bendix/King

Collins Avionics

Honeywell

Narco Avionics

THUNDERSTORM DETECTION SYSTEM MANUFACTURERS

These manufacturers' addresses can also be found in Sources.

B.F. Goodrich Flight Systems (Stormscope)

Honeywell

Insight Instruments (Strikefinder. This unit is currently out of production due to litigation by B.F. Goodrich. Current owners of Strikefinders installed prior to the litigation can have their units repaired by Insight, however.)

19
Stormscope
and Strikefinder

PILOTS HAVE KNOWN FOR YEARS THAT AN ADF NEEDLE CAN SHOW THE location of thunderstorms. Also well known is that radar's accuracy is limited for thunderstorm detection. Radar displays any weather containing moisture, which may or may not be associated with thunderstorms. Fortunately, a device that can "see" the noise generated by lightning strikes using similar principles as the ADF is available, making it possible for a pilot to spot thunderstorms and avoid the hazards of convective windshear and turbulence without having to install a complex and expensive full-blown radar system.

The device is called Stormscope, and it is now produced by B.F. Goodrich Flight Systems. Stormscope comes in two basic types: the three-part WX-1000-series with a CRT display, and the WX-900, which features a less-expensive super-twist liquid crystal display (LCD). The WX-900 has two parts, with the processor unit collocated in the indicator box.

STRIKEFINDER

Insight Instrument recently developed a similar system called Strikefinder, but has been enjoined from selling the unit in the U.S. due to a court injunction brought about by B.F. Goodrich. Insight is supporting Strikefinders it sold before the injunction took effect in February 1992, and the unit might be available in the future, so I will briefly outline some of its features in this chapter.

The Strikefinder also has its processor incorporated within the display case. Its range is similar to that of the WX-1000, but it is smaller and easy to install, with a prebuilt harness on which only one end must be terminated. Because of the Strikefinder's compact configuration and unique processing design, it is less susceptible to noise interference than the Stormscope, which was designed to receive frequencies in the 50-kHz range (slightly below ADF generators). In fact, the Strikefinder is virtually immune to onboard noise generators; it was designed to look at a broader frequency spectrum and detect only the sharp transients that form the activity inherent in lightning.

The Strikefinder is so precise that the system can tell the difference between reflected radiation and that which is the direct result of a lightning strike. The Strikefinder is quite light, thanks to its orange plasma display flat screen and self-contained processor.

STORMSCOPE

The lower-cost WX-900 lacks the power to detect lightning over 100-nmi from the aircraft. The WX-1000 has a 200-nmi range, which is practical during long-range flights where storms are in dynamic flux. If a storm is already brewing before a flight, the 100-nmi range of the WX-900 would be satisfactory, especially with a slower-moving aircraft. The faster the airplane, the greater the need for a longer-range lightning detector like the WX-1000.

The WX-1000 Stormscope is larger and heavier than the WX-9000 and has more features, including two views, either 360 degrees or a 120-degree view of forward airspace. The WX-1000+ system features gyro stabilization so weather information is displayed relative to the aircraft's heading, clock display, and the ability to interface with loran/GPS receivers and display navigation information on the Stormscope CRT.

The main advantage of the WX-1000 is that the CRT is easier to read because the CRT's intensity can be adjusted for various ambient light conditions.

Installation tips

The Stormscope's wiring harness is complex to assemble, from cutting wires and shield preparation, to careful harness routing. The completed harness is composed of three main subcables, each containing several smaller wires. Other wires are needed for gyro stabilization hookups (for the WX-1000+), and current requirements for the WX-1000 are higher than for the WX-900.

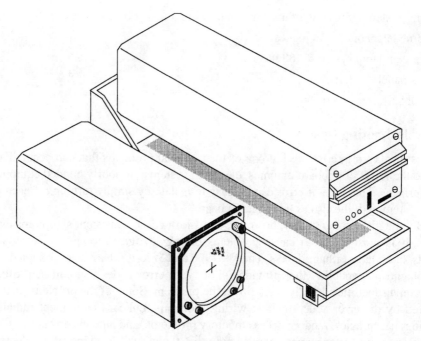

WX-1000 Stormscope system by B.F. Goodrich Flight Systems, composed of display unit (left), processor, and mounting rack.

The display unit (CRT) shouldn't be mounted within three inches of electric gyroscopic instruments like artificial horizons and turn coordinators. If so mounted, the effect might be a wobbling or vibrating display on the CRT.

Both the WX-900 and WX-1000 Stormscopes use the same antenna, a design similar to the combined loop/sense antenna used on ADF systems. Three coils of wire wound around a core form the directional heart of the antenna, which is the H-field component of the antenna (see chapter 7). A plate inside the antenna forms the E-field component.

An important consideration for Stormscope installations is the distance of the antenna from various noise-producing elements. Following is a list of such elements and the minimum distances these elements should be from the Stormscope antenna:

Cabling systems carrying five or more amperes—28 inches

VHF Comm antennas—14 to 24 inches

DME/transponder antennas—48 inches

ADF antennas—24 inches

Strobe light bulbs and power supplies—60 inches

Autopilot servos/trim servos/autopilot amplifiers—36 inches

Heating system igniters and fans, air-conditioning fans—60 inches

Airborne telephones—48 inches

Fluorescent lamp systems—60 inches

Access panels—26 inches

Control surfaces—36 inches

Troubleshooting tips

Strikes displayed in error are but one of the potential problems that can occur. These can be the result of onboard avionics, electrical systems, or poorly bonded equipment and surfaces. This type of error can be easy to isolate by simply turning off each aircraft system until the strikes no longer appear.

Bonding is another matter, however, and won't cause consistent symptoms every flight. It is most likely to cause problems during a flight through moisture-laden clouds, or on hazy or humid days. The WX-900 and WX-1000 units are designed with self-diagnostic capability that provides pilots with error codes that can help Stormscope repair facilities quickly track down the problem. Some of the problems that are covered by the error codes include wiring problems, onboard equipment radiation, heading inaccuracies, random access memory problems, and antenna errors.

Pilots using Stormscopes should know that the casual throwing of an electrical switch can cause a splash of strikes on the Stormscope screen, and so can taxiing over buried electrical cables. On older models, knowledgeable pilots will simply hit the Stormscope's reset button, but with later models, the Stormscope automatically resets itself.

The most important test to perform on a new Stormscope installation is the interference or ambient noise test, to ensure that nothing on board the aircraft is affecting the Stormscope's ability to function properly. This test should be performed will all engines running at the highest possible rpm and all aircraft systems functioning. Because it is possible for other aircraft to radiate their noise and interfere with your Stormscope, you might have to perform this test well away from other aircraft. Also, there should be no storm activity within 400 miles in any direction.

Following are some of the potential troublemakers:

- Poor bonding or grounds between equipment and airframe structure.
- Noise generators injecting RF directly into antenna.
- Degraded aircraft equipment radiating or inducing noise.
- Noise on DC line to Stormscope processor.

Aircraft systems most likely to cause the above problems include:

- Radios such as comm, DME, transponder.
- Motors, generators, alternators, inverters, servos, actuators.

- Strobe power supplies (poor design or failure of internal filtering system).
- Air-conditioning and heater fans and heater igniters.
- Fluorescent lighting systems.
- Windshield heat systems.

To begin the test, start the engines and warm them up, then run at full practical rpm with all aircraft equipment on, including the Stormscope. Once the Stormscope has initialized, strikes might begin to appear on the display. Reset the system and again observe the display for strikes. If the strikes return, turn the aircraft to a new heading and clear the screen. If the strikes reappear in the same location on the screen, ambient noise is causing the strikes. If the strikes are in a new location, they are probably due to a storm, if there is one within range.

Other isolated strikes that appear in small amounts can generally be ignored. The rule of thumb is that if the displayed isolated strikes are not clusters of strikes but are sporadically strewn around the screen, they should not present a problem as far as thunderstorm detection or presentation is concerned.

Run through the internal self-test provisions as specified in the user's manual. Covering the entire depth of material on self-tests is not practical in this book because of the number of varieties of Stormscopes models in the field. Note that comm radios can cause individual strikes to appear on the Stormscope. To prevent this problem, the Stormscope can be inhibited while transmitting on comm radios. Should two or more microphones be connected to the communications system, isolation diodes must be installed, and I recommend a Stormscope factory-authorized avionics shop for this job.

WX-900 troubleshooting

WX-900 troubleshooting covers three areas: the indicator (display/processor), the antenna, and wiring. If the display/processor does not turn on or show any signs of life, the problem is either in the display unit, internal processor, or the wiring. The first item to check before removing the unit for repair is that it is getting power and is properly grounded. Any mechanic should be able to perform this test. If power and ground check out okay, then the next step is to remove the display/processor and bring it to an authorized Stormscope repair shop.

WX-1000 troubleshooting

Following are some troubleshooting checks for the WX-1000. You can do some of these yourself, but many will require testing by a Stormscope repair shop.

- If the display presentation does not appear, the green LED will be illuminated. Check for proper power and ground at the processor. No power or a bad ground could be due to poor seating of the processor in the mounting tray, circuit breaker popped, broken wires to the mating connector, or a defective processor.

- If the green LED is faintly lit, the processor is getting power and is grounded, but there might not be power or a ground to the PWRSWHI and PWRSWLO connections. This could be due to broken wires, a defective processor, or the PWR/Brightness switch needs to be switched on.
- A bright green LED means the processor is getting satisfactory power, however, the display might be defective or the display wiring is open. It could also be as simple as the display connector being loose.
- Both green and yellow LEDs lit: this might be an overload to the processor or a system fault. The processor will have to be bench checked, and the wiring to the display and antenna will have to be examined.
- Green and red LEDs lit: this indicates the processor has a fault. The processor will have to be bench checked.
- Display distorted: the processor and display will have to be bench checked, plus the wiring in the display should be checked. The cause of the problem could be another panel-mounted instrument, such as electrically driven gyroscopic instruments.
- If the presentation appears to vibrate or wobble, it might be due to electrical or magnetic interference on the display. Isolate by turning off suspected components until the defect disappears. If this fails to resolve the problem, have the processor and display bench checked. With the Stormscope on and other aircraft instruments and systems running, you can slide the display unit out of the panel while it is still hooked up and watch for the wobble to disappear. If it does disappear, this confirms that the interference is coming from something nearby in the panel, most likely a device that projects a magnetic field. You can observe a similar effect by holding a telephone handset or a magnet near a computer screen.
- Improper brightness control may be observed as "blooming" of the image on the display. This might be a focus problem within the display and will require a factory-authorized repair.
- Incorrect information displayed on the "system data" screen is probably due to incorrectly installed option jumpers or a defective processor. This will require bench checking and factory-authorized repair.

It is important for you to know that troubleshooting recommendations for Stormscopes might require special test equipment, parts, and experience with problems specific to these unique lightning-detecting devices. This chapter is intended to raise some questions, discuss some hints on where the problem might be located, and hopefully help you get on the right track to solving some squawks without emptying your wallet.

MANUFACTURERS

B.F. Goodrich Flight Systems

Insight Instrument

20
Compass

IF YOU THINK YOU HAVE A PROBLEM WITH YOUR HEADING INDICATOR, check the accuracy of your compass first. This advice will save you lots of money.

Want to know how to make enemies with an instrument shop? Imagine their frustration when they find nothing wrong with an HSI or heading indicator that's been sent in because it precesses or displays the wrong heading. Their frustration builds even higher when they return the unit to the customer, and the customer complains, "It still doesn't work!" Over and over again, I've seen customers, mechanics, pilots, and kit builders send heading indicators in for repair. The instrument shop goes through the whole exercise and finds the bearing race is worn, possibly enough to cause precessing. Cautiously, for they've been through this many times, they warn the customer, "There is no guarantee this will solve your problem. There is a little bearing recessing, but it shouldn't be enough to cause the degree of error you described. Do you still want to have it repaired?" The customer says go ahead, the gyro is repaired, bench checked, found to meet factory specs, and sent back to the customer. The customer installs it, and the same squawk resurfaces.

The mechanic or owner calls the instrument shop and complains, "It's still doing the same thing." The instrument tech asks if the mechanic checked the indicator on an official compass rose or against a master compass. "Of course we have," is the defensive answer. The "defective" indicator is once again sent back, and the instrument shop finds nothing wrong but spends several hours trying to duplicate the squawk.

Finally, after being pressured by the instrument tech, the mechanic and owner taxi the airplane to a compass rose and check the compass. Sure enough, the compass was way off, and so was the heading indicator because the pilot set it according to the erroneous compass.

What do you suppose the customer will want now? You guessed it—they don't want to pay for the repairs to the heading indicator. After all, there wasn't anything wrong with it. But the instrument tech did exactly what he was asked to do, confirm a defect and repair it. In fact, he was instrumental (no pun intended) in determining the cause of the problem and pointing the way to a solution. In many cases, the instrument shop doesn't charge for this kind of repair, but it really is a lot to ask for; after all, it wasn't the instrument shop's fault. It is the troubleshooter's fault. The mechanic and/or the pilot should have taken the airplane to an official compass rose and confirmed whether the gyro or the compass was at fault. This isn't a rare occurrence, but sadly it happens more often than most can afford.

The same scenario happens with the customer trading in a perfectly good heading indicator for an overhauled unit. When the problem isn't fixed by the overhauled gyro, the owner gets upset, and whoever did the faulty troubleshooting is left with labor charges he has to swallow.

COMPASS CONSTRUCTION

The wet compass consists of a sensing elements (bar magnets) attached to a floating card that is free to move inside the compass housing. The compass card essentially stays still, always pointing in the same direction, while the airplane "moves" around the compass. The lubber line on the face of the compass is attached to the airplane and moves with the airplane, thus displaying the magnetic heading of the airplane. To dampen or restrict sudden changes in compass-card motion as the airplane moves around the card, the card is submerged in a fluid with a consistency similar to that of kerosene. Small compensating magnets allow for adjustments to keep the compass accurate.

Vertical card compasses

The vertical card compass is a replacement for the time-honored wet compass. The chief advantage of a vertical card compass, which is subject to the exact same errors as a regular compass, is the presentation. It looks and reacts just like a heading indicator, which makes using it much more intuitive.

Vertical card compasses have a massive magnet that is mounted on a shaft supported by jeweled bearings in vertical housing. As the airplane rotates, an azimuth card connected through gears to the magnet rotates to display the magnetic heading.

Remember that while the presentation is easier to interpret, the vertical card compass is just a compass and must still be calibrated regularly and is subject to normal compass errors.

COMPASS PROBLEMS

The main problem caused by compasses is when people ignore the need to calibrate the compass on a regular basis. After they've spent hundreds of dollars on unnecessary heading indicator overhauls, they learn that it is much cheaper to check the accuracy of the compass whenever they suspect a heading indicator accuracy problem.

Assuming the compass is in good shape physically, here is checklist for determining if the compass is the problem when you suspect the heading indicator is inaccurate:

1. Taxi the airplane to an official compass rose and turn on all normally used equipment (radios, lights, etc.). Keep the engine running.

2. With the airplane stationary, record compass deviation when you turn on intermittently used equipment such as electric prop deicer boots, electric fans, air-conditioner, etc. You need this information so that you know how far off your compass reads when you're using this equipment.

3. Turn the airplane to north (according to the compass rose) and set the heading indicator to match the compass. Note the reading on the compass, if it isn't exactly north. If the compass is more than 10 degrees off at this point, you need to calibrate it before continuing because the compass is out of legal limits.

4. Turn to east according to the heading indicator and record the magnetic compass reading.

5. Turn to south according to the heading indicator and record the magnetic compass reading.

6. Turn to west according to the heading indicator and record the magnetic compass reading.

7. Turn back to north according to the heading indicator. The magnetic compass should be within three degrees of what it read in step 3.

If the magnetic compass and the heading indicator match in step 7, the heading indicator is fine. Any errors more than 3 degrees (difference between the compass and the heading indicator) on the other cardinal headings are due to the compass, and the compass should be swung.

If when you turn back to north according to the heading indicator and the compass is more than 3 degrees different than north, you need to line back up on the north direction on the compass rose. After doing so, verify that the compass is reading the same as when you lined up on north in step 3. Note the heading indicator reading. If it is more than 3 degrees off from the compass reading, it is probably precessing too much. FAA standards call for no more than 3 degrees precession every 15 minutes, and if you've completed this exercise in less than 15 minutes and the heading indicator is more than 3 degrees off, then the gyro is due for some attention.

LOCATION

Each aircraft has its own unique magnetic pattern. The structure, control yoke, radios, engines, props, landing gear, and hardware all create magnetic influences, and these must be compensated for in order to obtain accurate information from your compass.

The factory location for your compass is usually the best place to put it. After all, the factory has determined that it's possible to obtain the necessary accuracy from that compass location. But over time, some things can change that will affect the compass and throw it off more than the allowable 10 degrees.

One problem that can happen on older steel-tube and fabric airplanes is that the steel fuselage gets magnetized over time. There is no way to prevent this, it's just a consequence of steel existing in a magnetic field (the earth's). If you had a big enough degausser (demagnetizer), you could theoretically demagnetize the airframe by running the airplane through the degausser. Attempts to demagnetize airframes using a portable degausser aren't so effective, because the magnetized area disappears where degaussed but then shows up somewhere else on the airframe. So what do you do if your airplane is hopelessly magnetized and you can't swing your compass to within 10 degrees?

The only option is to install either a remote compass whose sensor is mounted out on a wing away from the fuselage, or move the compass to an area where it is more accurate. I had this experience on a Citabria once. No matter how hard we tried, we couldn't get the compass swung within 10 degrees. The compass, by the way, was freshly overhauled. Finally, one of our brilliant mechanics came up with the idea of repositioning the compass. He experimented with various locations and was able to get great accuracy by moving the compass, normally mounted directly in front of the pilot on the top center of the glareshield, a few inches to the left of its original location. Problem solved, customer happy.

COMPASS REPAIRS

Unfortunately, compasses are another item that you aren't allowed to work on. In fact, you aren't even permitted to swing your compass, but you can do it under the supervision of a licensed mechanic. Please note that licensed A&P mechanics are not permitted to overhaul compasses because a compass is an instrument, and instrument overhauls are major repairs that can be done only by certificated instrument shops or by a licensed repairman. Sure, all the discount suppliers sell compass repair kits and compass fluid, but if you want legal components in your airplane, the compass overhaul must be done by an authorized shop. Compass removal and installation, of course, must be done by a mechanic or under a mechanic's supervision.

The flux valve (or flux gate) remote compass is mounted with three nonmagnetic screws to a mounting plate with three locknut assemblies. The valve is engraved to indicate "FWD," because the valve will only work correctly if properly aligned. Reference marks next to the "FWD" symbol are used during calibration to set the valve to correctly display magnetic headings on the compass card.

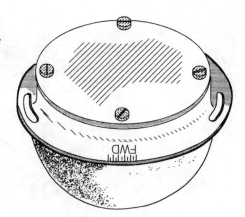

If your compass is starting to look yellow and the front glass is hard to see through, you might consider getting it overhauled, even if is still accurate. When you see bubbles in the fluid or when half the fluid is gone, it's not worth simply topping up the fluid because it's leaking from somewhere and the leak needs to be fixed. Over time, the gaskets that hold in the fluid get brittle and crack, and when you smell the kerosene odor of compass fluid, those worn gaskets are where it's coming from. It's time for an overhaul. After the overhaul or any installation of new equipment, the compass should be swung.

Don't forget that FARs require a working compass for any type of flying, so proper maintenance of the compass is essential. A nonworking or inaccurate compass is a no-go item.

COMPASS SWINGING

To swing the compass, you'll need to find an official compass rose. Don't use a compass rose that's been painted on the ground outside the maintenance shop. Compass roses have to be carefully designed and located in areas free of magnetic interference. Other criteria include using nonmetallic paint to draw the lines, proper radius for the size of aircraft using the pad, weight-bearing ability of the pad for use by large aircraft, and freedom from intermittent local disturbances such as nearby factories that use high current for short durations. If you're not sure of the quality of a local compass rose, ask the local FAA inspectors if the rose meets FAA Advisory Circular 150/5300-13, Appendix 4 specifications.

Next, you'll need a nonmagnetic nonferrous flathead screwdriver for adjusting the compass. You can make one easily by filing the tip of a piece of welding rod. Obviously, using a ferrous or magnetic screwdriver would make it impossible to adjust the compass's compensating magnets accurately, because each time you brought the screwdriver near the compass, the compass card would start spinning wildly. You might have seen this happen when you put your headphones on the dashboard next to the compass. In fact, it's a good idea to keep headphones away from compasses because the magnets in the headphones can permanently damage them.

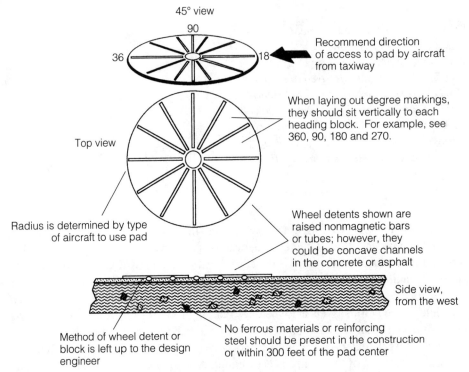

This illustration shows some of the requirements for an official compass rose.

Compass swinging is easier using two people—one to taxi the airplane and adjust the compass, and the other to stand outside and direct the airplane to the proper spot on the compass rose. It's hard to assess alignment of the airplane with the compass rose from inside the cockpit, unless the compass rose has detents against which you can stop your wheels when you are lined up. You can make the job easier, too, if the outside person has a hand-held transceiver.

Here's the step-by-step compass swinging procedure:

1. Taxi the airplane to the compass rose and line up so the airplane is pointing to magnetic north according to the compass rose. Make sure all radios and normal equipment are on, such as flashing beacon, strobes, and landing light (if you are in the habit of flying with it on all the time). Keep the engine running fast enough so that the generator stays on line. If it can be done safely, you might want to run the engine near the low end of the cruise range, usually around 1800 or 1900 rpm to more closely replicate actual flying conditions. Note that if you are swinging the compass on a taildragger, you'll need to rig up some way to keep the airplane in a level attitude while you swing the compass. An alternative method would be to swing the compass against a calibrated master compass while flying. Ask your avionics shop if it has a master compass.

2. Adjust the north-south screw on the compass so the compass card reads exactly north.

3. Taxi around and line the airplane up with east on the compass rose. You won't be able to simply turn right 90 degrees, you'll have to make a wide left 270 to get lined up on the compass rose properly.

4. Adjust the east-west screw on the compass so the compass card reads exactly east.

5. Taxi back around and line the airplane up with south on the compass rose.

6. Note the amount of deviation from south as shown on the compass. The aircraft is lined up with magnetic south according to the compass rose, but the compass will show some heading other than south, like 170, or 185, or 165.

7. Using the north-south adjusting screw on the compass, carefully remove half the deviation shown on the compass. If the compass reads 170 before the adjustment, turn the north-south screw so that the compass reads 175. The deviation is 10 degrees, and removing half the deviation brings the compass card 5 degrees closer to 180. If the compass reads 165, adjust the screw so the compass settles on 172.5 degrees.

8. Taxi to line up with west on the compass rose.

9. Note the deviation from west shown on the compass and remove half of it using the east-west adjustment screw.

10. Now you're ready to check the accuracy of the compass. Taxi back to north on the compass rose and note the deviation. It should be about the same as the deviation you obtained after adjusting the compass for south. If the south reading ended up being 5 degrees off, then you should see a 5-degree deviation on north. Remember, you're shooting for anything less than 10 degrees deviation on any heading. By making these four cardinal adjustments first, if they are below 10 degrees, then the compass should be within 10 degrees on all headings. Taxi to east and check the deviation there. Again, it should be about the same as the west deviation (after adjustment). If the north and east deviations are very different from south and west, you might need to make some careful, slight adjustments to the adjustment screws, but if the deviations are close, leave the adjustments alone.

11. On a piece of paper, note the 12 compass headings that are listed on the compass deviation card: north, 30, 60, east, 120, 150, south, 210, 240, west, 300, 330.

12. Starting with north, note the compass deviation at each point, with the airplane lined up on the proper magnetic heading according to the compass rose. Note the deviation either as a plus or minus from what the compass should read (+3, −2) or as the heading shown by the compass for a particular compass rose heading (92, 154, etc.), whatever suits your methods. I prefer the plus or minus

method because you add or subtract the deviation to your magnetic heading to obtain compass heading.

13. Fill out the compass correction card, note the date and the conditions (radios on, lights on, etc.), and install the compass card in the airplane.

14. Ask the mechanic or other qualified person who helped you swing the compass to make an airframe logbook entry and sign it. Make sure the logbook entry includes the deviations found during the swinging. That way, if you lose the compass correction card in the airplane, you won't have to swing the compass again. You can just make a new card using the numbers you so wisely entered in the logbook.

SLAVED COMPASS

Slaved compasses usually aren't affected by additional equipment because their sensing units are mounted well away from the cockpit in one of the wings. They should be checked for accuracy whenever you swing the compass. If inaccurate, the remote compass's flux valve or compass amplifier might need to be adjusted by your avionics shop.

Two frequent mistakes made with remote compasses are using magnetic screwdrivers to unscrew them from their mounting points in the wing, and reinstalling the compass backwards after a routine inspection. On Piper Seminoles, for instance, the remote compass is mounted to a right-wing inspection panel. A careless mechanic can easily remount the inspection panel 180 degrees off (the panel installs either way and isn't marked), and you'll only find out when you notice the compass card on the HSI is 180 degrees off next time you fly. If you have a remote compass installed in such a fashion, I recommend painting a stripe on one side of the panel so it's obvious which way the panel mounts to the wing. The panel should also be placarded: "Remote Compass: Do Not Use Magnetic Tools."

One word of caution: intermittently used equipment like windshield heat, prop de-ice, and heater fans can affect the compass. You should try each item separately and together and note how far off the compass is when these items are switched on. You don't want to calibrate the compass with these items on because they aren't used for normal flying, but you should be aware of how far off they will throw your compass so that you can compensate when using the equipment in IFR conditions.

COMPASS MANUFACTURERS

These compass manufacturers' addresses are listed in the Sources section of this book.

Airpath

Hamilton Instruments (vertical card)

Instruments & Flight Research

Precision Aviation (vertical card)

21
Gyroscopic instruments

GYROSCOPIC INSTRUMENTS INCLUDE TURN COORDINATORS AND HEADING, attitude, and horizontal situation indicators.

HEADING INDICATOR

The heading indicator, or directional gyro, is driven either electrically or by air blowing across a set of scoop-like paddles. The vertical compass card display visible to the pilot is driven through gears from the gimbal. Just as a toy gyroscope or top is resistant to movement once it reaches top speed, so is the gyroscope in the heading indicator. When the aircraft changes direction, the gyro maintains its position and the aircraft "turns" around the stationary gyro. Thus, the instrument's compass card shows that the aircraft is on a new heading. The jeweled bearings that compose the supporting mechanism for the gyro are very sensitive to any form of contamination such as dust and moisture, but if the air that drives the instrument is kept clean and at the correct flow rate, the heading indicator is a reliable and dependable instrument.

The primary problem with gyroscopic instruments is their tendency to precess. You'll notice this as the tendency of the heading indicator to drift off a chosen heading over a period of time. FAA specs call for no more than 3 degrees of precession each 15 minutes, and even with normal precession, you'll have to reset the heading indicator to match your compass every 15 minutes. If you have a slaved heading indicator or HSI, the indicator's compass card will automatically be kept lined up with the compass; your job becomes simply monitoring the heading indicator to make sure it matches the compass. Precession on air-driven gyros is caused by dirty filters, vacuum pump failure, or worn or damaged gyro bearings. Exceeding operational limits of the gyro such as degrees of pitch or bank can cause the heading indicator to spin crazily. This can also be caused by an internal failure of the gyro.

ATTITUDE INDICATOR

In order to fly IFR safely, pilots must have some way to discern the attitude of their aircraft. Without the attitude indicator and its ability to show the relationship between the aircraft and the horizon, the pilot is virtually cut off from the outside world.

According to the University of Southern California's book *Aviation Psychology*, a study of military aviators found that except during straight-and-level flight, the highest percentage of pilot eye fixation time was devoted to the attitude indicator. Although the airplane can be flown IFR without the attitude indicator, this instrument is essential to safe IFR operations.

The attitude indicator isn't too complex. It is essentially a gyroscope that is spun by airflow or electric power. The gyro spins in a double gimbal with the spin axis in a vertical plane. The fixed "airplane" symbol on the face of the instrument is attached directly to the instrument, which is in turn solidly fixed to the airframe. Thus the "airplane" symbol always does exactly what the airplane is doing, turning, climbing, etc. As the airplane changes attitude, the gyroscopic horizon remains parallel to the earth's horizon, and the pilot can discern the relative motion of the airplane by comparing the instrument's symbolic airplane with the fixed "artificial" horizon.

Information about the aircraft's attitude and changes in its attitude can be output to autopilots via potentiometers, contact points, LEDs, or even lasers. The autopilot uses these signals to make corrections to the aircraft's attitude as commanded by the pilot through the autopilot controls.

Modern attitude indicators have wide limits for safe operation, usually a maximum of 70 degrees pitch and 100 degrees of bank. Pushing the instrument beyond these limits can upset the gyro, resulting in the horizon bar swinging back and forth. Flying straight-and-level should eventually settle the gyro down. If your instrument has manual caging, engage this to settle the gyro down immediately.

Attitude indicator installation

Attitude indicators must be installed so that the instrument is accurate in a particular aircraft. Some aircraft panels, for instance, are not perfectly vertical, and the attitude indicator must be adjusted to reflect this. Adjustments to compensate for the tilt of the aircraft's panel are made by adjusting the instrument's rotor housing to match the earth's horizon. The instrument shop mounts the indicator to a tilt table set to the same angle as the aircraft's panel and aligns the rotor housing and pivot assembly for proper indication.

Backup gyro battery pack with built-in status lights. Often used in aircraft with a backup electrical attitude indicator. Always remember to turn off after use.

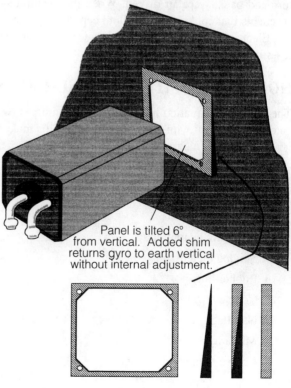

Mounting a gyro on a tilted instrument panel.

Panel is tilted 6° from vertical. Added shim returns gyro to earth vertical without internal adjustment.

Small roll adjustments are made on the airplane; most attitude indicator mounting holes are slotted to allow minor adjustments when installing the instrument. To get the setting correct, you might have to fly the airplane and have a mechanic make the adjustment while you hold the wings level. Or simply level the airplane on the ground using a long carpenter's level set on the control columns to show when the airplane is level on the ground.

Most air-driven attitude indicators don't have a warning flag to alert the pilot to incorrect indications. Sigma-Tek manufactures an attitude indicator with a warning flag, however. A warning flag is a good idea because it can be difficult to determine that the attitude indicator is failing (if you don't notice that the vacuum gauge reads zero). The indicator will start tilting as it spins down, and if you don't know the vacuum pump has failed, you might just try to follow the tilting attitude indicator until you notice that the other instruments aren't backing up what the attitude gyro is telling you.

TURN COORDINATOR

Turn-and-bank instruments and turn coordinators have a gyro suspended in the longitudinal axis that spins in alignment with the airplane's lateral axis. Most modern turn coordinators are electric-powered so as to provide a backup gyro instrument in case of vacuum-pump failure. Some notable accidents have occurred that could have been caused by the pilot's not realizing that all three of his gyro instruments, including the turn-and-bank, were air driven. When the vacuum system failed, so did the only instruments that could help the pilot keep the airplane right-side up.

Electric turn coordinators have a warning flag that lets you know if the instrument loses its electric power.

HORIZONTAL SITUATION INDICATOR

The horizontal situation indicator (HSI) combines two instruments: the heading indicator, and the CDI with glideslope needle. This makes the pilot's workload much easier and flying on instruments safer.

The typical HSI contains the following items:

- Compass card
- Heading flag
- Autopilot heading bug
- Slaving meter
- Lubber line
- Course arrow
- Nav flag
- Miniature airplane
- Course reciprocal pointer

- Left/right deviation bar
- Course arrow set knob
- Heading bug knob
- Glideslope flag
- Glideslope pointer or needle
- Deviation scale marks

Bendix/King KI252A HSI.

GYRO MAINTENANCE

Gyroscopic instruments don't require much in the way of aggressive maintenance beyond routine filter changes and gyro overhauls. Outright gyro failures due to internal wear usually occur after 1000 or more hours of gyro operation. If you're looking for a suitable time period for scheduling gyro overhauls so as to prevent failures rather than wait for them to happen, 1000 hours would be a good figure. If you don't fly that much and it takes years to accumulate that much time, every five years is a good interval for gyro overhauls and shouldn't add too much to your operating costs.

Bearing-to-race friction wear, inner or outer gimbal surface erosion, and heat all play a major part in internal component failure. Because proper gyro operation depends on minimum friction and an adequate flow of air, it doesn't take much to reduce efficiency. Minute particles of dust, tobacco smoke, and other contaminants can clog filters and reduce efficiency. Gyros are lasting longer these days, possibly due to the increased emphasis on the hazards of smoking, especially for pilots, but also due to improved cockpit housekeeping and careful handling of delicate gyros due to their high cost.

The easiest way to keep gyros healthy is regular filter changes. Most aircraft use a vacuum pump to suck air through the gyros. Before the air gets to the gyros, it goes through a large filter called the *central vacuum filter*. This is a fine filter that catches most particles and keeps them from getting into the gyros. You can tell if this filter is clogged by checking its color. Anything other than a clean, white appearance means the filter is ready to be changed. In an airplane owned by a smoker who smokes while flying, you'll see this filter turn yellow from the cigarette tar. The more clogged this filter, the harder your vacuum pump will have to work to provide the suction necessary to drive the gyros, and the shorter the life of the vacuum pump.

The central vacuum filter should be changed at least every 500 hours or once a year if the airplane doesn't fly that much. Vacuum pump manufacturer Airborne recommends changing the central vacuum filter whenever installing a new vacuum pump. But if you change the filter on a regular basis as suggested above, it might not be necessary to change the filter when changing the pump. Airborne's advice is probably due to the fact that many mechanics ignore the central vacuum filter and change it only when it looks dirty. Many aircraft, like Piper's Navajo, use enclosed canister-type central vacuum filters, and you can't evaluate the filter's condition by looking at it because the filter is inside a can. I worked on an airplane once where the suction was zero even though the vacuum pump was working. The central vacuum filter was so clogged that the pump couldn't suck any air through it. A new filter brought the system back to normal, although the vacuum pump had to be changed shortly thereafter because it had worked so hard trying to suck air through the clogged filter, so it wore itself out prematurely.

The other filter in the vacuum system is the vacuum regulator filter. This is installed at the vacuum system regulator and lets air into the system just before it goes through the vacuum pump to regulate the level of suction in the vacuum system. This filter isn't as critical to the instruments, but does prevent dirt from getting to the vacuum pump, so it is important for vacuum pump life. Replacement of this filter should be done every 100 hours, and the filter is cheap enough that it is worthwhile to replace frequently.

The rubber hoses that direct air to the gyros are important. Sluggish gyro operation could be caused by kinked or twisted hoses, and these should be inspected regularly, especially at the annual inspection. Excessive heat is a factor that can shorten gyro life. Expensive damage can happen to gyros in aircraft that sit outside without any protection from the sun. On a bright sunny day, the sun's energy passing through the windows creates a greenhouse effect, trapping hot air inside the cockpit. With each passing moment, heat levels rise, placing tremendous stress on everything inside the cockpit. This includes the electronic components in avionics equipment, nylon mounts, plastic housings, and even silicon lubrication inside indicators.

Problems caused by heat include tolerance variations from thermal expansion, resistance changes in electronic components, and thinning of lubricants. After the aircraft has been baking for an extended time, the pilot jumps into the cockpit, throws open the windows and doors and tries to cool the cockpit down. After starting the engine, the vanes in the gyros start to spin, but friction on the gyro's bearings is higher than normal. The result is a huge influx of gyro overhauls during the hot summer months.

The jeweled movements (bearings) used in gyros are made from artificial rubies and are extremely sensitive to shock and vibration. They can shatter if bumped hard enough. Gyroscopic instruments should be handled delicately. In fact, all instruments should be handled with great care. Some electrically powered instruments have jeweled movements, while engine instruments usually have simple brass bearing surfaces that aren't as sensitive. To be safe, handle all instruments as if they are more fragile than eggs. An egg can be dropped a quarter of an inch without damage. A gyro dropped the same height—which can impose up to a 20G load on bearings—won't show damage initially, but the damage will be evident later when you have to overhaul the unit prematurely.

Pilots and technicians should be aware of signs of gyro problems including excessive precessing, slowness to erect, spinning, or tumbling. Precessing is normally evident when the gyro spins up initially, and spinning or tumbling can occur during shutdown as the gyro slows down. Tumbling is an indication that the gyro is beginning to wear out and should be checked and repaired immediately. Spin-up usually takes about 1½ minutes and spin-down about 10 minutes. Be careful not to bump or bang the airplane while the gyros are spinning down because this can damage gyro bearings. After shutting down the engine, I recommend not moving the airplane until 15 minutes after shutdown. Move the airplane gently to avoid damaging gyros. Avionics systems should not be shut down until the airplane is completely stopped. Otherwise, electric gyros will start to tumble and bang around, possibly causing expensive damage.

Do not tap on gyros during shutdown, or any time, because this could cause flat spots on the bearings. Proper handling of gyros during removal and installation is important. For long life, gyros should be stored on soft materials like towels or bubble-wrap packaging. Vibrations from passing trucks, heavy feet, etc. can shorten stored gyros' lives.

When moving a gyro from the shop to the aircraft, the gyro should rest on a foam pad and not simply sitting on a hard cart or toolbox. If you see someone mishandling a gyro intended for your airplane, speak up and either refuse to have that gyro installed, or ask for a 1000-hour extended warranty.

GYRO TROUBLESHOOTING

Use these checklists to help isolate gyro problems.

Attitude indicator

Gyro shaking and spin-up during start should not exceed 1.5 minutes, assuming vacuum is set to proper level.

Gyro visual precessing (tilting away from level) during shutdown should last 5 or more minutes, and the gyro should still be spinning after the display has settled, for a total of 10 minutes after shutdown. Less than 5 minutes precessing and 10 minutes gyro spinning mean the bearings are worn, causing increased friction and a quicker shutdown.

During shutdown, the index pointer will swing partially across the horizon, dropping both right and left as it settles to the static position. This is perfectly normal.

In flight, the horizon should move smoothly in bank and pitch changes.

Continued wild shaking or tumbling of the gyro are signs of impending failure.

The wing-level pointer should not scrape against the moving parts of the instrument while the aircraft is pitching or banking.

Listen for unusual sounds such as a high-pitched whine, whistle, rumbling, or grinding noises. Grinding and rumbling indicate bad bearings. The high-pitched whine means the rotor is turning too fast, probably because the vacuum is set too high. A whistle indicates an air leak. A common place for this sound is around the shaft of the "airplane" symbol adjuster knob. Putting too much side pressure on the adjuster knob shaft can break the seal around the shaft, causing an air leak and the subsequent annoying whistling noise. The leak usually isn't enough to affect gyro operation, but it should be fixed because it can let contaminated air directly into the instrument, bypassing the filters.

If the autopilot is not following the gyro output, the pitch or roll pickoffs could be open or the contacts could be dirty.

Heading indicator

Compass card spinning means the gyro is tumbling. This can be caused by exceeding the pitch and bank limits of the instrument, or it could be a sign of imminent gyro failure.

If the compass card is intermittently pausing then rapidly catching up, it might be defective bearings or wiring in the compass synchro system.

Compass (directional) errors, could result from worn bearings, a gyro set to incorrect magnetic compass, a flux valve incorrectly calibrated or a remote defective compass, wiring problems with remote compass, ferrous fasteners near flux valve, flux detector bracket broken causing rotor to drag, or fluid leaking from flux detector.

Slave meter (on heading indicators slaved to remote compass) is hard left or right of center (remote compass failure). In this case, use the heading indicator as if it were not slaved and reset it every 15 minutes to match the wet compass.

Slave meter does not move from centered position. This problem could result from possible synchro system failure, the remote compass not being sensed. Use heading indicator as if not slaved.

Excessive spin-up time for gyro. Worn bearings, clogged filters, defective vacuum pump, or low power output (on electric gyros).

Autopilot is not following heading bug. Heading pickoffs are open or the contacts are dirty.

Heading indicator adjuster knob doesn't seem to work. This could be caused by the adjuster knob being too far forward on the shaft. To adjust the heading indicator, you must be able to push the knob in far enough to disengage the indicator's compass card from the rest of the instrument so you can reset it to match your compass. The knob is held onto the shaft with a small Allen-head screw, and the knob can be positioned farther or closer to the instrument on the shaft. If your airplane has a plastic false panel like most Pipers and some Cessnas, the instrument shop might have set the knob on the shaft too close to the instrument. When you install the heading indicator, then the plastic false panel, you might notice you can't adjust the heading indicator because the knob runs into the plastic panel before disengaging the gears inside the instrument. The solution to this problem is simple: adjust the knob so it sits farther back on the shaft and doesn't hit the plastic panel before disengaging the gears.

GYROSCOPIC INSTRUMENT MANUFACTURERS

See the Sources section for the addresses of these manufacturers.

Instruments & Flight Research

RC Allen

Edo-Aire

HSI/SLAVED COMPASS SYSTEM MANUFACTURERS

See Sources section for addresses.

Bendix/King

Century Flight Systems

Collins Avionics

S-TEC

Sigma-Tek

22
Radio altimeter

RADIO ALTIMETERS ARE FREQUENTLY AND INCORRECTLY CALLED RADAR altimeters. Radio altimeter transmissions aren't pulsed like radar signals. They are continuous, constant-amplitude frequency-modulated (FM) signals. The unit's transmitter/receiver computes the difference in frequency of the transmitted signal compared to the received signal. This difference is converted to height above ground. A knob on the front of the radio altimeter is used to select the decision height and to test the unit. When the aircraft reaches the selected decision height, the DH light illuminates and, with some systems, a horn sounds.

There are pitch and bank limits beyond which radio altimeter accuracy falls off. If you have a problem with your radio altimeter, make sure to note the altitude at the time of failure, weather conditions, and aircraft attitude.

INSTALLATION TIPS

When having a radio altimeter installed, finding enough real estate to mount the antenna can be a problem. The preferred spot is an area where a 120-degree cone is clear of obstructions such as other antennas, gear doors, spoilers, and other protuberances.

The transmitter/receiver mounts on the bottom inside fuselage skin, near the antenna. Make sure the installer mounts the antenna using nutplates so it can be removed from the outside, without requiring someone inside the airplane holding nuts while the other person unscrews the antenna-mounting hardware.

Two antenna types are generally available: one for horizontal mounting on a flat belly, and the other for mounting on "uphill" locations like the aft fuselage. The uphill antenna is internally skewed to compensate for the upswept angle of the tailcone. Proper antenna bonding is important for radio altimeter antennas.

Coaxial antenna cable should have sufficient room to prevent bends with a radius of less than 3 inches. Otherwise, reflected power can exceed specifications, resulting in reduced sensitivity.

RADIO ALTIMETER MANUFACTURERS

These manufacturers' addresses are listed in the Sources section of this book.

Bendix/King
Collins Avionics
Honeywell
Terra Avionics

Sources

SUPPLIERS

ACK Technology
440 West Julian Street
San Jose, CA 95110
(408) 287-8021

Acousticom
Champlin Industrial Park
28180 Clay Street
Elkhart, IN 46517
(219) 293-0534
Fax: (219) 294-7250

Aero Mechanism
20960 Knapp Street
Chatsworth, CA 91311-6161
(818) 709-2851

Aerosonic
1212 North Hercules Avenue
Clearwater, FL 34625
(813) 461-3000
Fax: (813) 447-5926

Aire-Sciences
216 Passaic Avenue
Fairfield, NJ 07006
(201) 228-1880

Airpath
13150 Taussig Avenue
Bridgeton, MO 63044
(314) 739-8117

Ameriking
20902 Brookhurst Street,
Unit 107
Huntington Beach, CA 92646
(714) 963-6977

Arnav Systems
22007 Meridian East
Graham, WA 98338
(206) 847-3550

Artex Aircraft Supplies
P.O. Box 1270
Canby, OR 97013
(503) 266-3959

Audio Com
395 Freeport #21
Sparks, NV 89431
(702) 331-2992

Aviall
7555 Lemmon Avenue
Dallas, TX 75209-0086
(214) 357-1811

Aviation Communications
1025 West San Bernardino Rd.
Covina, CA 91722
(818) 967-4183
Fax: (818) 332-7563

Aviation Crime Prevention Bureau
P.O. Box 3443
Frederick, MD 21705
(301) 694-5444

Becker Avionics
6100 Channingway Boulevard
Suite 303
Columbus, OH 43232
(800) 962-2094

Bendix/King
Allied Signal General Aviation
Avionics
400 North Rogers Road
Olathe, KS 66062-1212
(913) 768-3000
Fax: (913) 791-1302

B.F. Goodrich Flight Systems
2001 Polaris Parkway
Columbus, OH 43240-2001
(614) 825-2002
(800) 544-5759

Bose
The Mountain
Framingham, MA 01701-9168
(508) 879-7330 extension 4932
(800) 242-9008
Fax: (508) 872-8928

Brittain Industries
3266 North Sheridan Road
Tulsa, OK 74115
(918) 836-7701
Fax: (918) 836-7703

BVR Aero Precision
5459 Eleventh Street
Rockford, IL 61109
(815) 874-2471
Fax: (815) 874-4415

Century Flight Systems
P.O. Box 610
Municipal Airport
Mineral Wells, TX 76067
(817) 325-2517
Fax: (817) 325-2546

Collins Avionics
Rockwell International
400 Collins Road NE
Cedar Rapids, IA 52498
(319) 395-4085

Communications Specialists
426 West Taft Avenue
Orange, CA 92665-4296
(714) 998-3021
(800) 854-0547
Fax: (714) 974-3420

Comtronics
62 County J
Almond, WI 54909
(715) 366-7093

Concept Industries
2651 Pacific Park Drive
Whittier, CA 90601
(310) 699-0918

David Clark
360 Franklin Street
Box 15054
Worcester, MA 01615-0054
(508) 756-6216
Fax: (508) 753-5827

Dorne and Margolin
2950 Veterans Memorial Hwy
Bohemia, NY 11716
(516) 585-4000

Edo-Aire (see Sigma-Tek)

Electro-Voice
600 Cecil Street
Buchanan, MI 49107
(616) 695-6831

Emergency Beacon
15 River Street
P.O. Box 178
New Rochelle, NY 10801
(914) 235-9400

Evolution
18097 Edison Avenue
Chesterfield, MO 63005
(800) 859-9550

Flight Technology International
1571 Airport Road
Charlottesville, VA 22901
(804) 978-4359

Flightcom
7340 SW Durham Road
Portland, OR 97224
(503) 684-8229
(800) 432-4342
Fax: (503) 620-2943

Garmin
9875 Widmer Road
Lenexa, KS 66215
(913) 599-1515
Fax: (913) 599-2103

Hamilton Instruments
106 Neuhauf Street
Houston, TX 77061
(713) 644-0923

Honeywell Business & Commuter Division
5353 West Bell Road
Glendale, AZ 85308
(602) 436-8000

Icom America
2380 116th Avenue NE
Bellevue, WA 98004
(206) 454-7619

II Morrow
P.O. Box 13549
Salem, OR 97309
(503) 581-8101
(800) 742-0077

Insight Instruments
Box 194 Ellicott Station
Buffalo, NY 14205-0194
(716) 852-3217
(416) 871-0733

Instruments & Flight Research
2716 George Washington Blvd.
Wichita, KS 67210-1585
(316) 684-5177
(800) 373-7627
Fax: (316) 684-0140

Kollsman
4729 Palisade
Wichita, KS 67217
(800) 558-5667

Magellan Systems
960 Overland Court
San Dimas, CA 91773
(714) 394-5000
Fax: (714) 394-7050

McCoy Avionics
10761 Watkins Road
Marysville, OH 43040-9544
(513) 642-8080
(800) 654-8124
Fax: (513) 642-0220

MicroCom
Division of Microflight
Products
16141-6 Pine Ridge Road
Fort Myers, FL 33908
(813) 454-6464
Fax: (813) 454-6652

Mid-Continent Instrument
7706 East Osie
Wichita, KS 67207
(316) 683-5619
(800) 821-1212
Fax: (316) 683-1861

Narco Avionics
270 Commerce Drive
Fort Washington, PA 19034
(215) 643-2905
Fax: (215) 643-0197
or

P.O. Box 277
Laguna Beach, CA 92652
(800) 223-3636

Northstar Avionics
30 Sudbury Road
Acton, MA 01720
(508) 897-6600
Fax: (508) 897-7241

Oregon Aero
P.O. Box 5984
Aloha, OR 97006
(503) 649-4778

Peltor
63 Commercial Way
East Providence, RI 02914
(800) 327-6833

Pilot Avionics
24212 Solonica Street
Mission Viejo, CA 92691
(714) 474-0401

Plantronics
345 Encinal Street
Santa Cruz, CA 95060
(408) 458-4481

Pointer
1027 North Stadem Drive
Tempe, AZ 85281
(602) 966-1674

Precision Aviation
8124 Lockheed Street
Houston, TX 77061
(713) 644-7383

PS Engineering
9800 Martel Road
Lenoir City, TN 37771
(615) 988-9800
Fax: (615) 988-6619

**Puritan-Bennett Aero
Systems**
111 Penn Street
El Segundo, CA 90245
(213) 772-1421

**Radio Systems
Technology**
12493 Loma Rica Drive
Grass Valley, CA 95945
(916) 272-2203
(800) 824-5978
Fax: (916) 272-2362

RC Allen (no longer
manufacturing gyros,
used ones still available from
instrument
overhaul shops)

Ryan International
4800 Evanswood Drive
Columbus, OH 43229-6207
(614) 885-3303
(800) 877-0048
Fax: (614) 885-8307

S-TEC
946 Pegram
Mineral Wells, TX 76067-9594
(817) 325-9406
Fax: (817) 325-3904

Senheiser Electronics
6 Vista Drive
Old Lyme, CT 06371
(203) 434-9190

Sigma-Tek
1001 Industrial Road
Augusta, KS 67010-9566
(316) 775-6373
Fax: (316) 775-1416

Sigtronics
822 North Dodsworth Avenue
Covina, CA 91724
(818) 915-1993

Softcomm
2651 Pacific Park Drive
Whittier, CA 90601
(213) 699-0918
(800) 255-2666
Fax: (213) 692-8947

Sony
Sony Drive
Park Ridge, NJ 07656
(201) 930-1000
Fax: (201) 573-8608

Sporty's Pilot Shop
Clermont County Airport
Batavia, OH 45103
(513) 732-2593
(800) 543-8633

Telex Communications
9600 Aldrich Avenue
South Minneapolis, MN 55420
(612) 884-4051

Terra Avionics
3520 Pan American Freeway NE
Albuquerque, NM 87107-4796
(505) 884-2321
Fax: (505) 884-2384

TKM Michel
14811 North 73rd Street
Scottsdale, AZ 85260
(602) 991-5351
(800) 233-4183

Trans-Cal Industries
16141 Cohasset Street
Van Nuys, CA 91406
(800) 423-2913

Trimble Navigation
Avionics Division
2105 Donley Drive
Austin, TX 78758
(512) 873-9100
(800) 767-8628
Fax: (512) 345-9509

United Instrument
3625 Comotara Avenue
Wichita, KS 67226
(316) 636-9203
Fax: (316) 636-9243

Val Avionics
3280 25th Street SE
P.O. Box 13025
Salem, OR 97309-1025
(503) 370-9429
Fax: (503) 370-9885

Wag Aero
P.O. Box 181
1216 North Road
Lyons, WI 53148
(414) 763-9586
Fax: (414) 763-7595
(800) 766-1216
(800) 558-6868

MAGAZINES

Aviation Consumer Magazine
75 Holly Hill Lane
Greenwich, CT 06836-2626
(203) 661-6111
Fax: (203) 661-4802

Avionics Magazine
7811 Montrose Road
Potomac, MD 20854
(301) 340-2100

Avionics News
P.O. Box 1963
Independence, MO 64055
(816) 373-6565

Avionics Review
75 Holly Hill Lane
Greenwich, CT 06836-2626
(203) 661-6111
Fax: (203) 661-4802

Index

9909